Create React App 2 Quick Start Guide

Build React applications faster with Create React App

Brandon Richey

BIRMINGHAM - MUMBAI

Create React App 2 Quick Start Guide

Commissioning Editor: Pavan Ramchandani
Content Development Editor: Mohammed Yusuf Imaratwale
Technical Editor: Aishwarya More
Copy Editor: Safis Editing
Project Coordinator: Kinjal Bari
Proofreader: Safis Editing
Indexer: Manju Arasan
Graphics: Alishon Mendonsa
Production Coordinator: Shraddha Falebhai

First published: February 2019

Production reference: 1250219

Published by Packt Publishing Ltd.
Livery Place
35 Livery Street
Birmingham
B3 2PB, UK.

ISBN 978-1-78995-276-6

`www.packtpub.com`

To my wonderful wife, Nicole, for supporting me throughout the process of writing this book, and to my lovely daughters, Elaine and Amelia, who remain a constant light in my life. This is all for you!

– Brandon Richey

Contributors

About the author

Brandon Richey is software engineer and React enthusiast who has written a large number of popular React tutorials. He has been making professional and hobby programming projects spanning healthcare, personal sites, recruiting, and game development for nearly 20 years! When not programming, Brandon enjoys spending time with his family, playing (and making) video games, and working on his drawings and paintings.

About the reviewer

John Tucker has a broad development and soft-skills background. His recent focus has been all things JavaScript. He is an active writer on Medium.

Packt is searching for authors like you

If you're interested in becoming an author for Packt, please visit `authors.packtpub.com` and apply today. We have worked with thousands of developers and tech professionals, just like you, to help them share their insight with the global tech community. You can make a general application, apply for a specific hot topic that we are recruiting an author for, or submit your own idea.

Table of Contents

Preface

Create React App is, in my mind, the ultimate example of a proper bootstrapping tool. Instead of the multiple hours of tedium getting everything tweaked and configured to be just right and hoping that you haven't missed anything along the way, you are instead given a tool and a project that is built and ready to go from the first minute you want to start embarking on your project. Now, the start up time to get moving on a project that is fully-featured goes from hours, or maybe even days, to minutes, and nothing is stopping you from building the React project of your dreams!

This book is intended for those that want to get intimately familiar with the Create React App tool. We'll cover all of the commands, all of the new additions in version 2, and we'll cover actually building a project from scratch and touching on all of the key concepts along the way to make sure you're able to take advantage of this tool to the absolute fullest!

Who this book is for

This book is designed for anyone with some JavaScript knowledge who is looking to take better advantage of the Create React App bootstrap tool to get started building their own amazing React projects. If you're looking to get better at JavaScript and building projects with best practices in mind, this book will also be for you! Even if you're a React veteran who has just never or rarely used Create React App to get started with their projects, this book will still give you plenty to learn from and work with!

What this book covers

`Chapter 1`, *Introducing Create React App 2*, gets you started with Create React App and helps you to understand the prerequisites and commands you'll need in order to get moving!

`Chapter 2`, *Creating Our First Create React App Application*, establishes the foundations of the project that we'll use for the remainder of the book. This will cover the basics of setting up a Create React App project.

`Chapter 3`, *Create React App and Babel*, explains the latest changes that Babel supports and how to write superior modern JavaScript using the latest features.

`Chapter 4`, *Keep Your App Healthy with Tests and Jest*, delves into how to maintain a healthy software development life cycle by covering testing in detail.

`Chapter 5`, *Applying Modern CSS to Create React App Projects*, is where we'll learn modern techniques to make our projects look beautiful and keep our style sheets organized in a sane way.

`Chapter 6`, *Simulate Your Backend with a Proxy API*, experiments with building a pseudo backend to our project and introduces techniques for pulling live data from servers using Fetch.

`Chapter 7`, *Building Progressive Web Applications*, experiments with using service workers built into Create React App 2 in order to build a progressive web application.

`Chapter 8`, *Getting Your App Ready for Production*, is where we'll finish putting the application together, making it production ready, and creating a build that can be deployed to a production environment.

To get the most out of this book

You'll need to have some experience of setting up Node.js on your computer and of programming, and you'll also require a compatible code editor, preferably one that will show you the directory structure of your projects.

Download the example code files

You can download the example code files for this book from your account at `www.packt.com`. If you purchased this book elsewhere, you can visit `www.packt.com/support` and register to have the files emailed directly to you.

You can download the code files by following these steps:

1. Log in or register at `www.packt.com`
2. Select the **SUPPORT** tab
3. Click on **Code Downloads & Errata**
4. Enter the name of the book in the **Search** box and follow the onscreen instructions

Once the file is downloaded, please make sure that you unzip or extract the folder using the latest version of:

- WinRAR/7-Zip for Windows
- Zipeg/iZip/UnRarX for Mac
- 7-Zip/PeaZip for Linux

The code bundle for the book is also hosted on GitHub at `https://github.com/PacktPublishing/Create-React-App-2.0-Quick-Start-Guide`. In case there's an update to the code, it will be updated on the existing GitHub repository.

We also have other code bundles from our rich catalog of books and videos available at `https://github.com/PacktPublishing/`. Check them out!

Download the color images

We also provide a PDF file that has color images of the screenshots/diagrams used in this book. You can download it here: `https://www.packtpub.com/sites/default/files/downloads/9781789952766_ColorImages.pdf`.

Conventions used

There are a number of text conventions used throughout this book.

`CodeInText`: Indicates code words in text, database table names, folder names, filenames, file extensions, pathnames, dummy URLs, user input, and Twitter handles. Here is an example: "At the very top of the `App.js` file, we're going to add our `import` statement."

A block of code is set as follows:

```
const App = () => {
  return <div className="App">Homepage!</div>;
};
```

Any command-line input or output is written as follows:

```
$ yarn add bootstrap@4 reactstrap@6.5.0
```

Bold: Indicates a new term, an important word, or words that you see on screen. For example, words in menus or dialog boxes appear in the text like this. Here is an example: "Select **System info** from the **Administration** panel."

Warnings or important notes appear like this.

Tips and tricks appear like this.

Get in touch

Feedback from our readers is always welcome.

General feedback: If you have questions about any aspect of this book, mention the book title in the subject of your message and email us at `customercare@packtpub.com`.

Errata: Although we have taken every care to ensure the accuracy of our content, mistakes do happen. If you have found a mistake in this book, we would be grateful if you would report this to us. Please visit `www.packt.com/submit-errata`, selecting your book, clicking on the Errata Submission Form link, and entering the details.

Piracy: If you come across any illegal copies of our works in any form on the internet, we would be grateful if you would provide us with the location address or website name. Please contact us at `copyright@packt.com` with a link to the material.

If you are interested in becoming an author: If there is a topic that you have expertise in, and you are interested in either writing or contributing to a book, please visit `authors.packtpub.com`.

Reviews

Please leave a review. Once you have read and used this book, why not leave a review on the site that you purchased it from? Potential readers can then see and use your unbiased opinion to make purchase decisions, we at Packt can understand what you think about our products, and our authors can see your feedback on their book. Thank you!

For more information about Packt, please visit `packt.com`.

1
Introducing Create React App 2

This book will be a guide on how to effectively use **Create React App** 2 (**CRA**) to create a new React project and build the web project of your dreams! We will cover many topics, including how to install Create React App, the project structure you get by default, and how to add code and libraries to your project. We will explore everything you'll need to be able to build complex, modern web applications using the latest and greatest of the most common React project configurations and compilations.

To be able to do this however, we first need to take a little time to talk about the project itself, its humble beginnings, and what problems it is ultimately attempting to solve. By understanding the history and the intention, we can better understand how to take full advantage of the toolset we are provided and also understand where and why limitations exist.

In this chapter, we'll discuss what Create React App is and what it brings to the table. By the time you're done with this chapter, you'll understand why Create React App is so important and how it helps the developer get more done in less time overall. We'll also discuss what topics the book will cover, the format itself, and how to best follow along.

In this chapter we will be looking at the following topics:

- Starting a new Create React App project
- The commands for starting and stopping your server
- The commands for running tests
- The commands for creating production-ready builds
- The commands for exiting the Create React App confines to further tune and configure your project

What is Create React App?

A lot of different programming languages, tools, and frameworks have a number of different ways to jumpstart development for their particular toolset. Sometimes this requires downloading a bunch of libraries, or getting started with a pre-built binary file or compressed archive for the right architecture, operating system, or other configurations. Sometimes it has a nice pre-built pathway to get started in a way that minimizes frustration but potentially limits available options.

The trouble, however, is that with a lot of JavaScript frameworks, there was not a similar option. Getting started using any particular framework or technology was actually a markedly difficult problem to solve, due to differing combinations of every person's skill set, operating system, and task.

Create React App is JavaScript 's answer to the *getting started* toolset that did not exist in any particularly approachable way. Generally speaking, to get started with a project, you'd have to learn a large number of supporting technologies and techniques before you could really get moving. You'd have to know a configuration framework, such as Babel, Webpack, Brunch, or Gulp. As well, you would have to know how to get a project structure going in JavaScript. After you've figured everything else out, you'd have to learn how to set up a development server that auto-reloads changes on the fly. After all of that, you still have to figure out how to set up your testing framework, React, and any additional libraries you want.

This ends up being a huge amount of effort, and that's just to get started. It's compounded by the fact that every single piece of framework and configuration that you're developing expertise with might not transfer into your next job!

Instead, Create React App aims to do something different: make configuration and setup a one-step process. This allows you to focus on getting started and building your application earlier, and worry about the more in-depth portions of work later. You can focus more time on writing your code and less time on configuring a great development environment. Your environment in a Create React App application will already be a great development environment, and that's a fantastic removal of barriers and obstacles for developers, both new and seasoned!

The **Command-line interface** (**CLI**) tool provides a great development environment that encourages rapid iteration and test-driven techniques. We have a lot of the configuration and specific libraries figured out for us so we don't have to do that legwork. Moreover, you're never locked in to any choices you make. The Create React App team included an **eject** option that pulls the entirety of the application you've been developing and turns it into a standard webpack or babel build, for example, that can be plugged into anything compatible with **Node Package Manager** (**NPM**). You don't have to be worried about having to duplicate a huge amount of effort to transfer your code from Create React App to your own project or a specific environment configuration and setup at your job; you can just make something that transfers nicely, safely, and cleanly. You can even tweak the configuration at this step (after ejection) and further make this application your own!

What is the history of Create React App?

To better understand where Create React App succeeds, we have to understand where the JavaScript development world started. We need to see the warts of the system to know why certain things were fixed and how they were fixed. Let's talk a little bit about the history of JavaScript development and some of the main issues that developers were running into frequently!

The early days of JavaScript development

To start, you need to dive back into the past of dealing with JavaScript code in the frontend. For a long time, you would end up with these JavaScript files that you'd just download off of a **content delivery network** (**CDN**) somewhere, throw into your frontend code, write a bunch of extra JavaScript code in front of that, and call it a day.

This was nice in the sense that you had your dependencies locked down to whatever version you downloaded and stuck on the server, and whatever you deployed was pretty easy to develop against because all of the dependencies were already there and ready to go. Unfortunately, it introduced a ton of problems in many other ways. For one, you would run into issues constantly where one of the libraries you downloaded was completely incompatible with a specific version of one of the specific versions of another library, and often that was a complex and difficult process. The way most people solved that problem was divided into a few camps:

- Going through and finding all of the incompatibilities and fixing them
- Writing complex glue code that would make the libraries behave together by wrapping one of the libraries and providing a means for the two libraries to work together

- Downloading a different version of the library just for another library and storing them separately, resulting in giant JavaScript bundles when you load the web page because you're probably downloading two to three different versions of something, such as jQuery

Yes, that last bullet point is a real thing that real developers did! You can probably see why this is something developers tried to move away from as soon as they could.

The bundle era

To solve this problem, it was important to solve the dependency problem in general. The move toward Node.js-based tools, such as `npm`, helped significantly, because now your dependencies would be pulled from a centralized location and versioning became a first-class citizen of JavaScript development, which was fantastic!

What was less fantastic, however, was when you needed to apply this problem to browser code and rich web applications. Often, this meant an intricate dance of understanding what libraries were required for which projects. If you wanted to use React with JSX (we'll talk more about this later), as well as the latest JavaScript syntax, you needed to know exactly what versions of React and Babel to include. You'd also need to understand which Babel plugins you'd need to have to support your use of whatever draft of JavaScript syntax.

Do you want to use some CSS transformers or any other language help, such as TypeScript or Flow, in your React project? If so, building and configuring your project becomes markedly more difficult, and we haven't even gotten to the problem of getting this code put together to be used on the browser! Now you needed to have a wide breadth of knowledge just to get your project started, and a wide depth of knowledge for knowing how to set up and configure something such as Webpack, Bundler, Grunt, Gulp, or Brunch!

This is the point of development that we were in before the prevalence of command-line tools and configuration utilities, so let's dive into that by talking about what problems Create React App solves!

What problems does CRA solve?

Create React App is designed to solve the problem of needing to understand a large number of different tools, scripts, configuration utilities, configuration languages, and file types just to get started developing. So now this isn't a problem you need to solve when you're advanced in your project and learning. And it isn't a problem you need to solve when you're an expert and trying to optimize your bundle to minimize what the end user needs to download when they want to use your fancy web application!

Remember, the problem we're talking about here is not one that the experts are solving alone: this problem existed at all skill levels of development and for every person. What's worse, these problems were duplicated every time you started a new project. As developers, we hate duplicating and wasting effort, so the Create React App team set out to remove these speed bumps!

Create React App allows you to get started at any skill level, at any level of comfort and familiarity with JavaScript and its ecosystem. You can start a project and get everything you need, including testing tools and frameworks, with a single command-line tool.

It is not laziness. It is *efficiency*.

It is not oversimplification. It is *removing barriers*.

Installing prerequisites for Create React App

First and foremost, you'll need to have `npm` installed on the computer that you're working on. Without that, there's no way to install the prerequisite libraries and projects. You can download Node and `npm` for your project at `https://nodejs.org`, then perform the following steps:

1. Find the appropriate installer package for your computer and operating system for Node and NPM at `https://nodejs.org` and follow the instructions provided by the installer.
2. Install an appropriate code editor or **Interactive Development Environment (IDE)**. I've had the best experiences with Visual Studio Code, so that gets my personal recommendation, but you can use anything you're comfortable with!
3. Once you've installed Node and `npm` (if you haven't already), you're ready to go!

Now that everything is set up, working, and installed to the version that we need, we can start iterating! One of the fastest ways to learn a project is to start building it and iterating on it as we learn more, so we're going to do exactly that.

Creating our first Create React App project

You should begin by picking a primary `Development` directory that you want all of your development work for this book to take place in. Wherever that directory is (I'm always a fan of a `Development` directory somewhere in my `home` folder or `Documents` folder), you'll then create a new project. This will be a throwaway project, since we're going to instead focus on playing around with Create React App and getting comfortable with starting from a blank project. Let's create a new project, which we will call `homepage`.

For this throwaway project, we'll pretend we're writing a fancy `homepage` replacement. You can actually pick whatever sort of project you want, but we will be throwing this preliminary project away after this chapter. After you build your project, you should see the following output:

```
$ npx create-react-app homepage

Creating a new React app in [directory]/homepage.

Installing packages. This might take a couple of minutes.
Installing react, react-dom, and react-scripts...
[... truncating extra text]
Done in 13.65s.

Success! Created hello-world at [directory]/homepage
Inside that directory, you can run several commands:
  yarn start
    Starts the development server.
  yarn build
    Bundles the app into static files for production.
  yarn test
    Starts the test runner.
  yarn eject
    Removes this tool and copies build dependencies, configuration
files
    and scripts into the app directory. If you do this, you can't go
back!
We suggest that you begin by typing:
  cd homepage
  yarn start
Happy hacking!
```

Those instructions that we see after successfully creating a project are critical to our workflow in Create React App. By default, there are four main commands (and a large number of options) bundled into Create React App. Also, if you are using `npm` instead of Yarn, note that a lot of the comments and output in the Create React App CLI help pages refer to Yarn primarily. Now, these commands (`start`, `build`, `test`, and `eject`) are relatively self-explanatory, but it is still important to dive a little further and learn a bit more about them.

A quick look at the options of CRA

Before we can dive into building out the app of our dreams with Create React App, we'll have to start by analyzing each of the commands that come with Create React App and what each of them do, plus when to use each command!

Each of the commands corresponds with a specific part of the software development life cycle: building the application, running a development server, running the tests, and deep customization and configuration. Let's explore each of the commands in greater detail!

The yarn start command

The function of this command is to *start the development server*.

Running `start` on your Create React App project will bring your project from code to your web browser. That is to say, it will take your project's code and compile everything together. From there, it will load a development server with a default starter template. The other nice thing about this is that it will actually pick up any changes you make to any code (assuming you save that code), so you don't have to constantly play the game of make a change, save the file, restart the server, refresh the browser; instead, you will have instant feedback for any of the changes that you make.

Starting off with a completely fresh Create React App project and running `start` will yield the following:

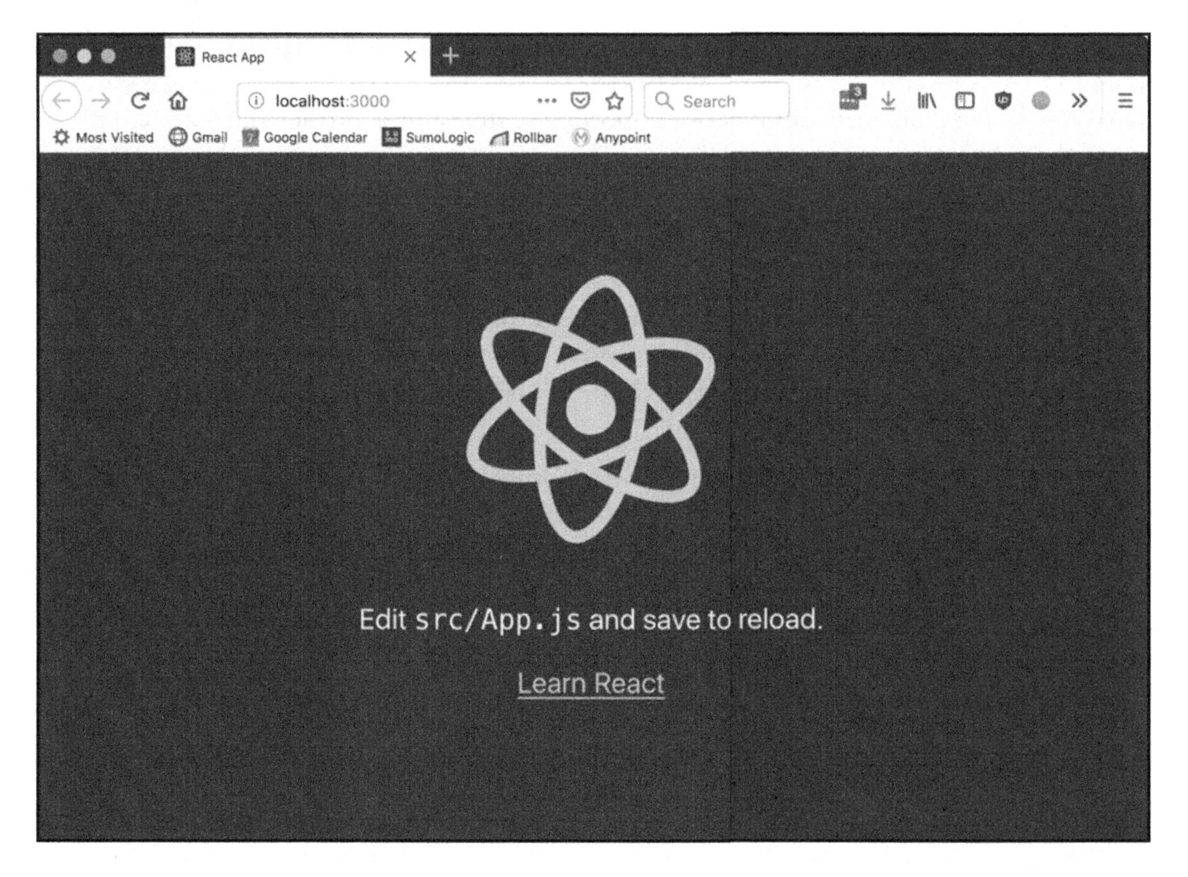

The yarn build command

The function of this command is that it *bundles the app into static files for production.*

Running `build` takes the application and turns it into something more production-ready. What does that mean? Well, if you're already pretty comfortable with what tools such as webpack and brunch do in terms of turning them into production sites, you basically already know what this accomplishes. If, on the other hand, this all sounds incredibly confusing to you, I'm going to take a little bit of time and explain it in slightly less vague terms.

Essentially, most browsers can't handle code written for Create React App projects just by default. There is a lot of work that needs to be done in taking the code and translating it into something that makes more sense for the browsers, ensuring that it doesn't need to rely on help to interpret everything. From there, the code is also minified! It shrinks things down by renaming functions and variables, removing white space where it can, and doing small optimizations here and there until the code is reduced to a very clean and usable version. Everything is compressed and the file is condensed down as much as it possibly can to reduce the download time (which is important if you're targeting a mobile audience that may not have great internet speed).

Minified means exactly what it sounds like. It is the condensing of code into much smaller values, making it unreadable to humans but highly digestible for computers!

The yarn test command

This function *starts the test runner.*

Running `test` does exactly what you'd expect it to do: runs all of your tests for your application. By default, when you spin up a new project with Create React App, your project will include many extra tools that should all be ready for you to start hacking away at the tests. This is especially helpful if you choose to approach a more test-driven development approach to your project, something that can be incredibly useful in a frontend development world.

The first time you run `test`, you should see some output on your screen that may look a little like this:

```
 PASS  src/App.test.js
   renders without crashing (18ms)
Test Suites: 1 passed, 1 total
Tests:       1 passed, 1 total
Snapshots:   0 total
Time:        1.976s
Ran all test suites related to changed files.
Watch Usage
 › Press a to run all tests.
 › Press f to run only failed tests.
 › Press p to filter by a filename regex pattern.
 › Press t to filter by a test name regex pattern.
 › Press q to quit watch mode.
 › Press Enter to trigger a test run.
```

Even better than all of this being built and provided to you is all of the options and additional tools that you get along the way for this! Getting a test framework set up and running consistently in your application can be a major pain in the neck, so having this figured out for you makes your life a thousand times easier. On top of all of this, the test watcher that comes with Create React App projects will also watch and live-reload on changes made to any related files, similar to the `start` command.

These are just the defaults. It's worth taking a look at some of the extra commands that come along with our test watcher:

- `Press a to run all tests`: Like the command says, if you press *A* in that window, it will just decide to run every single test in your project from zero and output the results. Use this if you need it and need to verify a fully-green test suite at any time.
- `Press f to run only failed tests`: I speak from personal experience when I say setting something such as this up in the past was an absolutely dreaded task. This is great when you're taking an approach of *red, green, refactor* in your project and want only the tests that failed last time and are just trying to get those to pass. You can use this as part of your development methodology to slowly clear away the cruft of your application's failing tests until you're back to all of them passing!

Red, green, refactor: This refers to a common pattern of development where you write your tests first with the intention of them failing, then write the minimum amount of code to make them pass, then refactor the code until they break again, and repeat the cycle. While this is usually used in an interview context instead of real-world development, the process itself is very much a real-world process.

- `Press p to filter by a filename regex pattern`: This is a very cool bit of functionality. Let's say you modified some code that affected all functionality related to users, but you have a giant test suite and don't want to test the entire thing. You could instead target all user code by hitting *P*, and then typing in `user` and seeing what tests run.
- `Press t to filter by a test name regex pattern`: Similar to the previous option, but this goes a step further by looking at what your tests are named (more on this in a later chapter) and runs tests based on those descriptions instead of by the filenames the tests are located in.

- `Press q to quit watch mode`: There is not much to explain here; this will quit the test watcher.
- `Press Enter to trigger a test run`: Pressing *Enter* will just redo whatever your last test was, which is very helpful when you're using one of the regex pattern options but don't want to have to retype the pattern every single time.

The yarn eject command

Removes Create React App scripts and preset configurations and copies build dependencies, configuration files, and scripts into the app directory. If you do this, you can't go back to using Create React App on your project!

For this one, it is worth taking a look at what the documentation says for this command. In layman's terms, this turns your project from a Create React App project, turns it into a Webpack configuration, and removes a lot of details of Create React App and the React Scripts project that essentially hides some of the details from you. A similar concept would be buying a computer pre-built versus assembling it yourself (or reassembling it). You may start off wanting everything all put together for you, but maybe some day you'll want to add some more RAM or replace the video card, at which point you'll have to open up what was previously a black box to enable you to configure things further!

This is also something you might do if you need to go outside of the confines of the default project structure and configuration that you get from a base project. This will allow you to turn it back into a standard Webpack project and add new libraries, change the defaults and baseline details, or go even further and swap out other core components.

Let's explore the created project

Finally, we should take a little time to see what precisely gets created and thrown into your project.

Create React App will start off by generating a README for your project called `README.md`. This is a markdown-formatted file that tells other people how to use your project effectively (or, if you're like me, it reminds you a few months down the line how to use all of the tools and tricks you've implemented in the project down the line).

You will also get a **favicon**, which is that little icon that shows up next to your website path in the address bar, and is used for any bookmarks to your application down the line. Next, we have the public or `index.html` file, which is the primary workhorse that includes all of your fancy React code, and more importantly, tells the web browser where to render your React application to; in our case, we have a `div` element that acts as the main target for React to render to. The source of the file is, by default, as follows:

```
<!DOCTYPE html>
  <html lang="en">
    <head>
      <meta charset="utf-8">
      <link rel="shortcut icon" href="%PUBLIC_URL%/favicon.ico">
      <meta name="viewport" content="width=device-width, initial-scale=1,
shrink-to-
       fit=no">
      <meta name="theme-color" content="#000000">
      <!--
        manifest.json provides metadata used when your web app is added
to the
        homescreen on Android. See
        https://developers.google.com/web/fundamentals/web-app-manifest/
      -->
      <link rel="manifest" href="%PUBLIC_URL%/manifest.json">
      <!--
        Notice the use of %PUBLIC_URL% in the tags above.
        It will be replaced with the URL of the `public` folder during
the build.
        Only files inside the `public` folder can be referenced from the
HTML.
        Unlike "/favicon.ico" or "favicon.ico",
"%PUBLIC_URL%/favicon.ico" will
        work correctly both with client-side routing and a non-root
public URL.
        Learn how to configure a non-root public URL by running `npm run
build`.
      -->
      <title>React App</title>
    </head>
    <body>
      <noscript>
        You need to enable JavaScript to run this app.
      </noscript>
      <div id="root"></div>
      <!--
        This HTML file is a template.
        If you open it directly in the browser, you will see an empty
page.
```

```
          You can add webfonts, meta tags, or analytics to this file.
          The build step will place the bundled scripts into the <body>
tag.
          To begin the development, run `npm start` or `yarn start`.
          To create a production bundle, use `npm run build` or `yarn
build`.
        -->
      </body>
    </html>
```

I mentioned a `div` element that acted as the main React render target: the `div` with an `id` of `root` acts as our primary render target and is the critical component to make your application function. Remove this and your application will not render correctly in the browser anymore! Following that, there is the `package.json` manifest file. This stores all of the dependencies that your project uses, plus some of the metadata used to describe your project (which might include the name, the version, the description, or some other pieces of metadata). We also have a `yarn.lock` file if you're using Yarn, which locks down the list of libraries and dependencies that your project is using in a way that prevents your project from randomly breaking when one of those libraries updates.

All of your project's dependencies, libraries, and things that make it tick behind the scenes live in the `node_modules` directory. This also brings us into the `src` directory, which is arguably the most important directory in our entire project structure! It is where all of the work that we're going to be doing—all of the source code—will live.

Inside of that directory, we have our `index.js` file, which handles our main render call for React, supported by a package called `ReactDOM`. This takes in our `App.js` component, which is our primary root-level component, and tells React where that needs to get rendered to back in that `index.html` file I showed you earlier.

We also get a little bit of style by default with an `index.css` file. This is the base-level style sheet that our project will use and we'll be configuring on top of.

In terms of our non-test code, `App.js` is the final component that we get through Create React App by default. What is in there is not particularly important to us, because we're just going to remove all of the code in that file and start over anyways! `App.css` stores the style sheet for that component, which allows us to make sure that any style included for each component can be stored and configured independently of each other. We're also given the React logo in the form of a **Scalable Vector Graphics** (**SVG**) file, which is the React logo (`logo.svg`). We don't need that, so feel free to delete it!

`serverWorker.js` is a file that tells our app how to exist/function as a service worker for a **Progressive Web App**, but we'll dive into this in a later chapter where we focus specifically on progressive web applications!

Finally, we have the only pre-built test for us. The `App.test.js` file contains the suite (not a suite, I suppose, since it's only one test, but it will become a suite over time) of tests just for our `App.js` component. That's it! That's the default project structure for our Create React App project!

Adding code to our project

One of the easiest ways to understand the default project structure is to actually get in there and start messing around with things, so let's do precisely that! We'll delete some of the default code that comes with our project and start building things up ourselves to get a good feel for how the project should be structured and learn how each file interacts for when we start playing around and changing the file structure!

Creating our first component

To create our first component, follow these steps:

1. Open up the newly-created project in your favorite text editor, and run the `start` command in that project as well to bring up the browser window to see the results of any changes we make along the way.
2. Let's do something all developers love to do: delete old code!
3. Once in the code, we can work through the main primary ways to work with React in the latest JavaScript syntax changes that are included in Babel. Given that, let's take a look at the ways to work with React classes. We can either use functions, or we can use classes to introduce React code to our code base. We'll start off with just using functions and over time incorporate classes as well, and we'll discuss how, when, and why to choose each along the way. Granted, either creation method requires React regardless of the implementation method, so we need to actually import it at the start of our code.

4. At the very top of the `App.js` file, we're going to add our `import` statement:

```
import React from 'react';
```

This line tells JavaScript that we want to `import` the React library, and that we can find the React class from the `react npm` library (Create React App obviously already included that for us). This gives our code the React support that we need, plus it adds support for JSX templates, and everything else we need to be able to write base-level JavaScript !

5. With our imports out of the way, let's write up our first bit of code:

```
const App = () => {
 return <div className="App">Homepage!</div>;
};
```

Here, we're diving a little further into some new JavaScript syntax that you may not be used to if you're coming from the older JavaScript world. The previous line is responsible for creating something called a constant function, which limits our ability to redefine or modify the `App` function after the fact. This function that we're writing doesn't take any arguments and always returns the same thing. This is a functional component, so we need to write the `return` statement to return out a JSX template that tells React how to render our React component to the browser. We also make sure to tell React that our main component should have a CSS class name called `App`.

The `className`, not `class`! Class is a reserved keyword in JavaScript , so that's why React needs this one little gotcha!

6. At the end of this code, we'll need to add an `export` statement to enable other files (such as our `index.js` file, specifically) to be able to import the right modules into our code base:

```
export default App;
```

Our end result is that when our browser refreshes, we should see **Homepage!** pop up on the screen!

Wait, what is JSX?

You may not know what JSX is, but if you do, feel free to skip this. Otherwise, I'm going to provide a very quick summary for you!

To put it simply, JSX is just a mixture of JavaScript and HTML that functions essentially as a templating language. This is a bit of a simplified explanation; JSX is actually some smart syntax wrappers around calls to `React.createElement`, but put together in a way that more closely resembles HTML. This way, we can write interface code that is incredibly similar to HTML, which allows developers, designers, and others to work with our code (assuming they're already comfortable working with HTML), but we also get access to a few extra features since it is a JavaScript -based templating language.

The first bit of functionality that we get is that we can actually embed any JavaScript statements inside of any JSX by wrapping it in curly brackets! A gotcha to this, though, is that we need to remember that JSX is JavaScript first, and as a result there are some words and syntax here and there are are reserved (class being the prime example of this), so there are specific variations you'll need to use when writing JSX (such as `className`).

Embedding style sheets in our component

Working with React and creating these nice browser-based interfaces is great, but without any kind of styling in place, the whole thing is going to look pretty plain overall. The good news is that Create React App also provides you a nice framework for cleaning up your interfaces as well! Right now, since we deleted a bunch of code, we currently should have an entirely blank `App.css` file. We'll need to head back to the `App.js` file and add the following line to the top to make sure it includes our new `App` component style sheet:

```
import "./App.css";
```

This will tell React to make sure the `App` style sheet is included as part of our component's style sheet. If `App.css` remains empty, though, that won't amount to much, so let's also change our default style sheet to something a little more interesting:

```
.App {
  border: 1px solid black;
  text-align: center;
  background: #d5d5f5;
  color: black;
  margin: 20px;
  padding: 20px;
}
```

Save the file, head back to your browser window, and you should see something similar to the following:

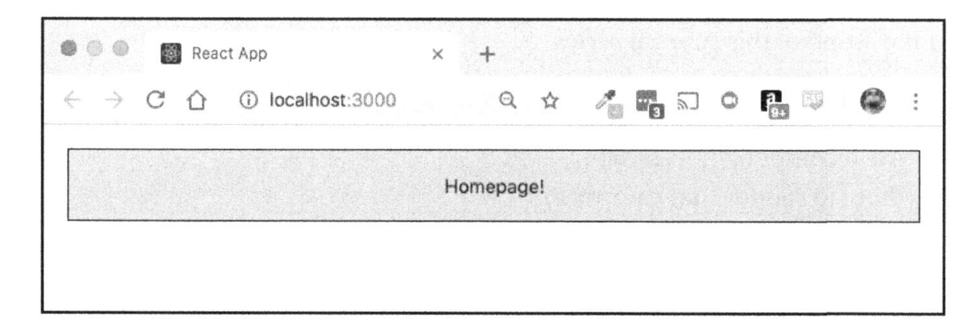

Okay, we have some code that functions now, and that's a good place to start in our application, so we'll hop over to `index.js` and quickly figure out precisely how the component gets into the browser. Open up `src/index.js`:

```
import React from 'react';
import ReactDOM from 'react-dom';
import './index.css';
import App from './App';
import * as serviceWorker from './serviceWorker';
ReactDOM.render(<App />, document.getElementById('root'));
// If you want your app to work offline and load faster, you can change
// unregister() to register() below. Note this comes with some
pitfalls.
// Learn more about service workers: http://bit.ly/CRA-PWA
serviceWorker.unregister();
```

At this point, we've seen `import React` already. The previous line imports `ReactDOM` (which houses the main `render()` function) that we need to be able tell React what component to render, and where to render it to! This comes out of the separate `react-dom` `npm` module.

After that, we have another style sheet included, this time being `index.css`. This will function as our global, baseline CSS file. After that, we `import` our `App` component (remember our `export` statement that we wrote earlier?) with `import App from './App'`. Note that we can leave the `.js` off completely, and that we include a dot and a slash in front of the name of the file; this tells Node that we're importing something from our local file system and not from an NPM module instead! `App.js` lives as a `local` file inside of our `src` directory, so the local include suffices.

We end with a new line, `import registerServiceWorker` from `./registerServiceWorker`, which allows us access to implementing service workers for progressive web apps in our Create React App. Progressive web applications are a bit outside of the scope of this tutorial series.

`render()` is a function call that takes two simple arguments:

- Which component to render
- Where to render that component

Since our component name was imported as `App`, and because we're using JSX, we can treat `App` like an HTML tag:

```
<App />
```

Remember, all tags in JSX need to be closed, whether via shorthand syntax such as in the preceding example or longer syntax such as following:

```
<App></App>
```

The final piece to our rendering puzzle is that we need to figure out where in the DOM the React component is that we need to render to, through the `document.getElementById('root')` line. This tells JavaScript that it needs to find an element on the page with an `id` of `root`, which will end up being our rendering target!

There we are! We have an admittedly basic, yet still a full start, application in React that we wrote in almost no time at all, and we had no stress or headaches trying to set up our development server, figure out which libraries we needed, make the code and browser window auto-reload, or, well, you get the idea.

Seriously, what more can a developer ask for?

Looking forward – what will we do?

What more can we ask for? Well, a lot, actually! In the next chapters, we'll go more into depth as we get comfortable with the development workflows afforded to us through Create React App. Let's explore the plan for this project that we're going to be building (since the **hello-world** application was just an opportunity for us to play around with things and won't be our final project going forward).

The project plan

Over the course of this book, we will build an application entirely using Create React App, encompassing a number of common modern React development techniques, methods, and best practices. We will spend time exploring the different libraries that are available and how to best utilize them in our Create React App project and with minimal effort too! We'll build a project that will take advantage of the very best of modern JavaScript development, taking advantage of the latest features of Babel and React. We'll use the most recent syntax changes in JavaScript to their full effect! We will make sure our application is fully tested and bulletproof, keep it beautiful with CSS modules and **Syntactically Awesome Style Sheets** (**SASS**), and even simulate the backend server so that we won't even need a separate backend server just to do development!

Finally, we'll explore how to make our application work online or offline through service workers, and then top off our application by getting it production-ready, and making our application minimized, clean, and deployable!

Summary

In this chapter, we explored the options that are made available to us when we're starting up a Create React App project. We also spent a good amount of time exploring the history of frontend development before Create React App, and even got a little bit of time to sit and put together a nice little starter application as an exercise in exploring the default project structure.

You should now feel much more comfortable with Create React App, the default project structure, and the language constructs that will enable us to get more work done in the later chapters, so without any further ado, let's charge ahead and start building a more complex application, which will serve as the basis for each chapter for the rest of our project.

2
Creating Our First Create React App Application

In `Chapter 1`, *Introducing Create React App 2*, we started off by taking a good, long look at Create React App and some of the options it provides. We even got started with `create-react-app` and started learning React at a very basic level. What we need to do now, however, is start diving into building an application that will serve as the framework for adding more functionality and testing the limits of Create React App.

To make things extra easy, we're going to build a simple **to do list**, since that is an application that nearly everyone can understand. It even has a great non-digital analog to it, making it a simple thing to reason about!

In this chapter, we'll cover the following topics:

- Designing a web app
- Building a simple project structure
- Passing values to components via props
- Passing functions to children components via props
- Basic component styling with included CSS

Creating our first major project

It's now time for us to move forward and start building a real project that will function as the baseline project for all of the other features that we want to explore in this book! To do that, though, let's take a brief moment to talk about how we want to design our application.

Designing our application

It's very difficult to build a project when you're not sure precisely what you're building in the first place, right? When we talk about how to design, build, and plan an application, we need to talk about the problem we're ultimately trying to solve in the first place. With that in mind, let's talk about the theoretical vision for our application.

First off, we're going to build out a mixture between a **pomodoro tracker** and a to-do list. This will give us the functionality of a plain old to-do list, but also allow us to track time spent on each item as we go through the list. We'll keep the overall design of this application pretty simple; there's no reason to dive into a giant application. A relatively small and simple application will teach you all you need to get started quickly with Create React App.

This chapter is also going to be the only chapter that's really only focused on the React side of things and less on Create React App. Being able to get started with any tool is essentially useless if you don't know how to build something after you get up and moving, so that is what this chapter is designed to help you solve.

Our application will have a simple to-do interface with a **Mark As Done** button for each. For each item, you'll be able to mark the item as complete after you add it and it will change the display of that item to let you know it's done. There's not really anything particularly fancy going on, just a very simple application design. Let's take a look at what the design for this might look like (at a very high level):

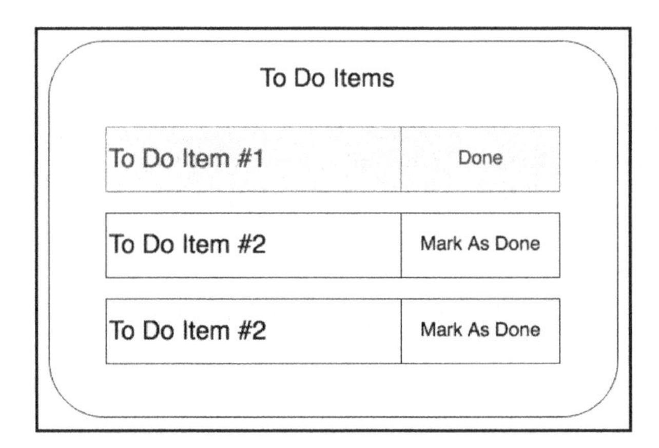

Building the baseline functionality for our application

Now that we understand the design, we'll want to jump right in to creating the project and getting things built. While the application is not particularly tricky, there's a decent amount of complexity overall and a pretty good amount of code we'll end up having to write. To make things work, we'll separate out our application's concerns and make sure what we're building, even in its limited scope, is still very similar to what you'd build in a real world application!

Creating our project

Similar to the previous project, we'll start off by creating a new project with Create React App, which we'll call `todoifier`:

```
$ create-react-app todoifier
```

After the project has been created, we'll also verify that everything was set up correctly and runs by running `start` on the project:

```
$ yarn start
```

Initializing our components to build on top off

Whenever you're building your project, you should strive to keep the top-level component, which is `src/App.js` in our case, as simple as possible and keep as little code in it as you possibly can. In our case, we're just going to remove everything (similar to the work we did in the previous chapter, `Chapter 1`, *Introducing Create React App 2*) and replace it with a simple replacement header and not much else:

```
import React from 'react';
import './App.css';

const App = () => (
 <div className="App">
   <h2>Todoifier</h2>
 </div>
);

export default App;
```

We'll also want to remove everything from `App.css`, since we're taking a blank-slate approach with this project as well!

Building separate components in separate files

One of the nicest things about Create React App is how simple it makes even the process of importing other files as their own separate React components without you really having to think about how Webpack is organizing everything. We're going to build a new simple component to get started with. Let's create a `Todo` component to keep track of each of the `Todo` items we'll need to add as we go along.

Back over in `src/Todo.js`, we'll want to duplicate everything from `App.js` (except the string in the `className` property and the function name):

```
import React from 'react';
import './Todo.css';

const Todo = () => <div className="Todo">I am an item</div>;

export default Todo;
```

There's nothing exciting to talk about here, so we'll keep forging ahead! We should also create a `Todo.css` file to make sure our component does not remain unstyled:

```
.Todo {
  border: 2px solid black;
  text-align: center;
  background: #f5f5f5;
  color: #333;
  margin: 20px;
  padding: 20px;
}
```

Without doing anything, we won't see the results of our fancy new `Todo` component that we just created, so we'll need to head back to `src/App.js` and change the code. We'll start by adding an `import` statement at the top for the `Todo` component! Remember, we're loading this file from the local filesystem and not some installed dependency:

```
import Todo from './Todo';
```

We'll also need to include the `Todo` component somewhere in the source so that it shows up when we re-render the page:

```
const App = () => (
  <div className="App">
    <h2>Todoifier</h2>
    <br />
    <Todo />
  </div>
);
```

All we've added here is the `Todo` component, which is getting rendered in the main root `div` of the `App` component. When the browser refreshes (assuming you've saved), you should see the `Todo` component show up and be ready to go!

The exciting part of this whole process is that we've already introduced better code standards and reusability by doing this. The `Todo` component has been fully extracted out, so if we wanted to include multiple `Todo` components in our `App`, we could do so without having to do anything more complicated than copying and pasting a few lines of code.

This sounds pretty great, so let's try it out ourselves and verify that it all works as we expect. Back in the `App` component, add a few more `Todo` components as JSX tags:

```
const App = () => (
  <div className="App">
    <h2>Todoifier</h2>
    <br />
    <Todo />
    <Todo />
  </div>
);
```

When we have our `Todo` declared twice in the root of our `App` component, we should see those two show up:

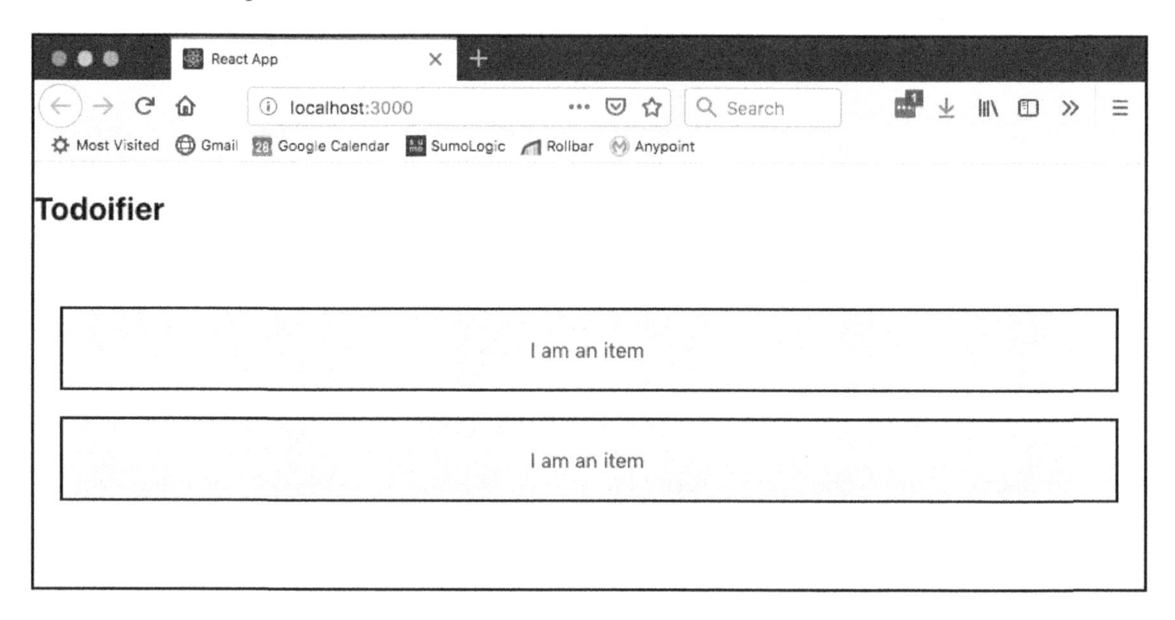

With that, we've gotten a nice clean amount of reusability and have had to put in almost no effort! The problem that still exists, though, is that there is no variation here. The components are just blindly repeated over and over, and we'd much rather this do something such as display some different content per each `Todo`. We can make that work in React by introducing two new concepts: **state** and **props**! We'll get to state in a little bit, so let's start off with props to get this all implemented in the simplest way possible.

Introducing props

So, what are props? Props are shorthand for *properties*, and as you can guess, they define properties inside of our React components. Generally speaking, these get passed in from the parent, although they can get passed in from anywhere, truth be told.

Right now, we're just using a simple functional component, and that function doesn't specify any arguments as part of its signature, so if we want to start using props we'll have to change that first.

Let's open up our Todo component in src/Todo.js, and change the function declaration to also pass in a props argument:

```
const Todo = props => {
```

This would roughly be the equivalent of us writing the following in vanilla JavaScript:

```
function Todo(props) {
```

Next, we'll have to change the display text to actually use something from our props argument, so we'll add a reference to {props.description}:

```
const Todo = props => <div className="Todo">{props.description}</div>;
```

Save the file, because now we'll have to head back over to our primary App component (src/App.js) and start passing in the description as part of the properties passed in to our Todo components:

```
const App = () => (
  <div className="App">
    <h2>Todoifier</h2>
    <br />
    <Todo description="Do the thing" />
    <Todo description="Do another thing" />
  </div>
);
```

After saving the file and seeing the browser window refresh, we should expect to see the properties we just entered now show up in the browser, as follows:

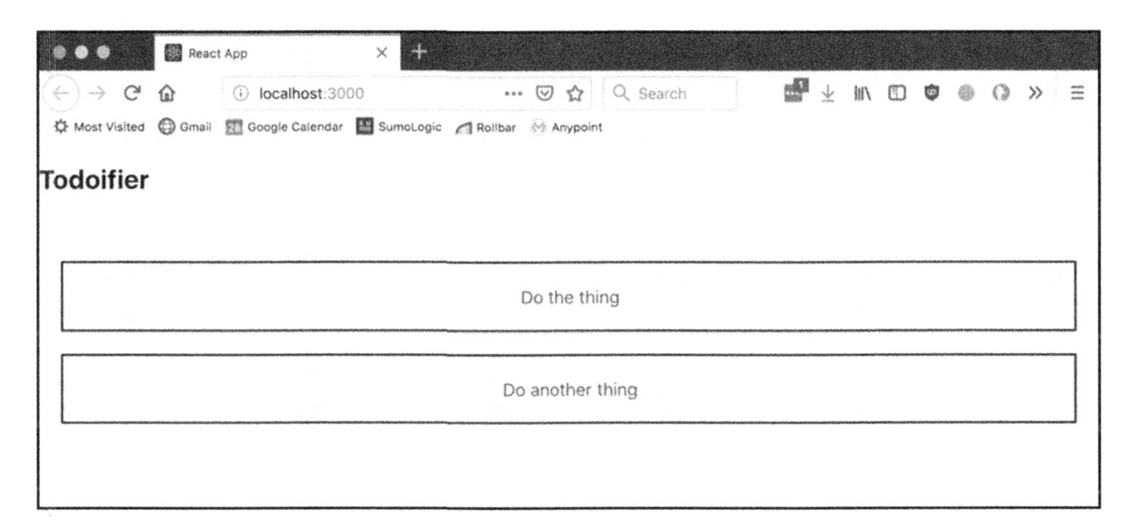

And there we are! Reusable, modifiable components, done with almost no effort at all!

The even better part is that any changes to `props` will trigger React to re-render that component (depending on what changed and where it changed). This is something that is profoundly useful, especially when you factor in that the old world had you checking for changes, and then trying to either delete and recreate elements on the fly or try to sneak the changes in without having to remove it all away.

Props are great, overall, but if we want to do something a little more permanent and something that is better for storing how something changes over time, we need to introduce the concept of state. Instead of props, state is meant to be used for something that is changing all of the time, generally local to a single component; you'll pass the state down to child components that need it via props.

The trouble is that we're currently using functional components, which is fine for now, but the minute we want to start tracking any sort of internal state, we'll need to switch to a different method of creating our React components.

Writing a class-based component

In **ECMAScript 6** (**ES6**), we got our first taste of real object-oriented programming in JavaScript with **Classes**. A class is declared in a fundamentally different way than our functional components, but most of the core tenets remain the same and there's not a huge amount more we need to learn to start using them.

The first thing we'll need to do is make a small modification to the `import` statement in `src/Todo.js`. We'll need to `import` not just React itself: we'll also need to `import` a particular named export specified in React, something called `Component`. Let's take a look at what the new `import` statement looks like:

```
import React, { Component } from 'react';
```

We have our `Component` imported as well, so let's explore the syntax for declaring a `class`:

```
class Todo extends Component { /* ... */ }
```

This tells JavaScript that we're building a new `Todo` class that inherits the functionality of `Component` (thus the `extends` keyword). Next, any React component we build as an ES6 class needs to have a `render()` function declared. To declare a function inside of a class, you just write the name, the arguments, and then the body inside of your class definition:

```
functionName(argument1, argument2) { /* ... */ }
```

React specifically requires us to declare a `render()` function with no arguments, as we mentioned earlier. Our `return` statement is identical to what we had in our previous functional component, so putting everything together we should end up with something similar to this:

```
class Todo extends Component {
  render() {
    return <div className="Todo">{this.props.description}</div>;
  }
}
```

Here, we write out our `render() { ... }` function, which is largely unchanged except for one small change: `props.description` is now `this.props.description`!

The reason for this is that props is not something that is just an argument on a function anymore. It's actually part of a class-specific property, so we need to tell JavaScript that when we say `props`, we actually mean the *props local to this class*. We just shorthand that with `this.props`! With that out of the way, we can start diving even further into the world of state!

Bringing state into our component

Part of declaring state to a class component is to start off with an initial or default state. We can't do that without telling JavaScript what to do when our class is actually instantiated, so our class will need to have a `constructor` to handle that work. In our `Todo` class, we'll build out our `constructor` function, which will take in `props` as its single argument:

```
constructor(props) {
  super(props);
  this.state = {
    description: props.description,
    done: false
  };
}
```

JavaScript knows to use `constructor()` as our constructor since that is a language construct, and we know it needs to take in `props`. Since we're extending off of React's `Component` class, we need to call `super()` as our first line of code in `constructor()`. This tells JavaScript to instead use the code in `constructor()` of `Component` to set up whatever it needs to. Next, we set the state by declaring a new variable attached to our class called, uninterestingly enough, `this.state`. We make it a plain object with a key of `description`, which just stores the passed-in description on the `props` argument. It also has a property called `done` that starts off with a default value of `false` (since we should not create our tasks as already done). This code by itself won't actually do anything, so let's also change our `render()` function to take advantage of our `state`:

```
render() {
  return <div className="Todo">{this.state.description}</div>;
}
```

Nothing has quite changed yet. Instead, we'll need to add some form of interactivity to make the case for using `state` really known!

Adding interactivity via state modifications

We'll add a very simple `button` to our `Todo` component called `Mark as Done`. When clicked, this `button` should change our `state done` status for that `Todo` item to `true`. Now, we'll want to make sure that anything that does change is only changed on this component and not all components, which is a big part of using internal state! Let's first build out our `markAsDone()` function:

```
markAsDone() {
  this.setState({ done: true });
}
```

That being done, we can move on to implementing our functionality by including our `Mark as Done` button:

```
render() {
  return (
    <div className={'Todo' + (this.state.done ? ' Done' : '')}>
      {this.state.description}
      <br />
      <button onClick={this.markAsDone}>Mark as Done</button>
    </div>
  );
}
```

Now, if we just hit save, wait for the refresh, and try to click the `markAsDone` button, we'll end up getting an error message:

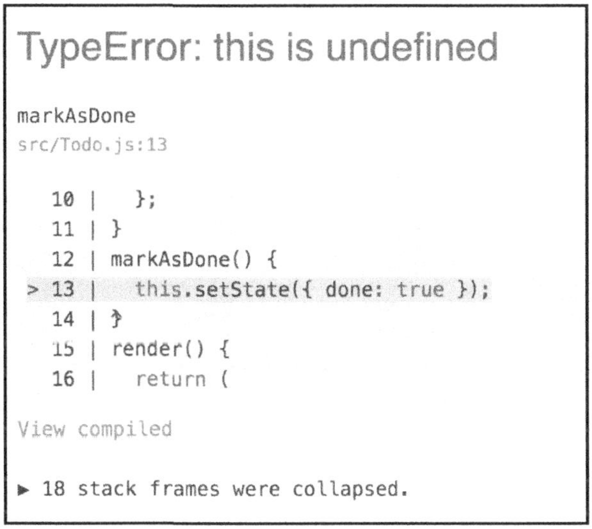

```
TypeError: this is undefined

markAsDone
src/Todo.js:13

  10 |   };
  11 | }
  12 | markAsDone() {
> 13 |   this.setState({ done: true });
  14 | }
  15 | render() {
  16 |   return (

View compiled

▶ 18 stack frames were collapsed.
```

Let's explore this error message a little more. We're getting a **TypeError: this is undefined** message, here, and it's not the most clear error message in the world, certainly. This is one of the drawbacks of using ES6 classes with any sort of React component in combination with JavaScript event handlers. So in this case, when we have our `onClick` calling out to `this.markAsDone`, and the function goes into the body of `markAsDone`, it tries to call `this.setState` but it doesn't actually understand what `this` is trying to reference! This only happens with event handlers, so we don't need to worry about this all of the time. The good news is that there is a simple means of fixing this issue. Let's add one more line back to our `constructor`, as follows:

```
this.markAsDone = this.markAsDone.bind(this);
```

This tells JavaScript that if it ever sees a reference to `this` inside of the `markAsDone` function, it is a specific reference to the `Todo` class. Save the file and click the **button**—it works! Well, you can't tell whether it works yet. We'll need to add a little bit of visual indication that it has worked.

Indicating our state with CSS

We're very close to this working perfectly, but we're missing a little bit of code to tell our React component to know when to use certain CSS classes. Let's start by adding a new function, `cssClasses()`, which will return a list of CSS classes to include in our component:

```
cssClasses() {
  let classes = ['Todo'];
  if (this.state.done) {
    classes = [...classes, 'Done'];
  }
  return classes.join(' ');
}
```

There's nothing particularly special about this other than the use of the JavaScript spread operator (the `...classes` bit). This is just a way for us to add on to the end of the array in a safe way. Next, we'll change the logic where we declare `className` for our component to use this new function:

```
  render() {
    return (
      <div className={this.cssClasses()}>
// ...
```

Finally, in `src/Todo.css`, add the new `.Done` CSS class definition:

```
.Done {
  background: #f58888;
}
```

And now, we can see the result when we click on one of the **Mark as Done** buttons:

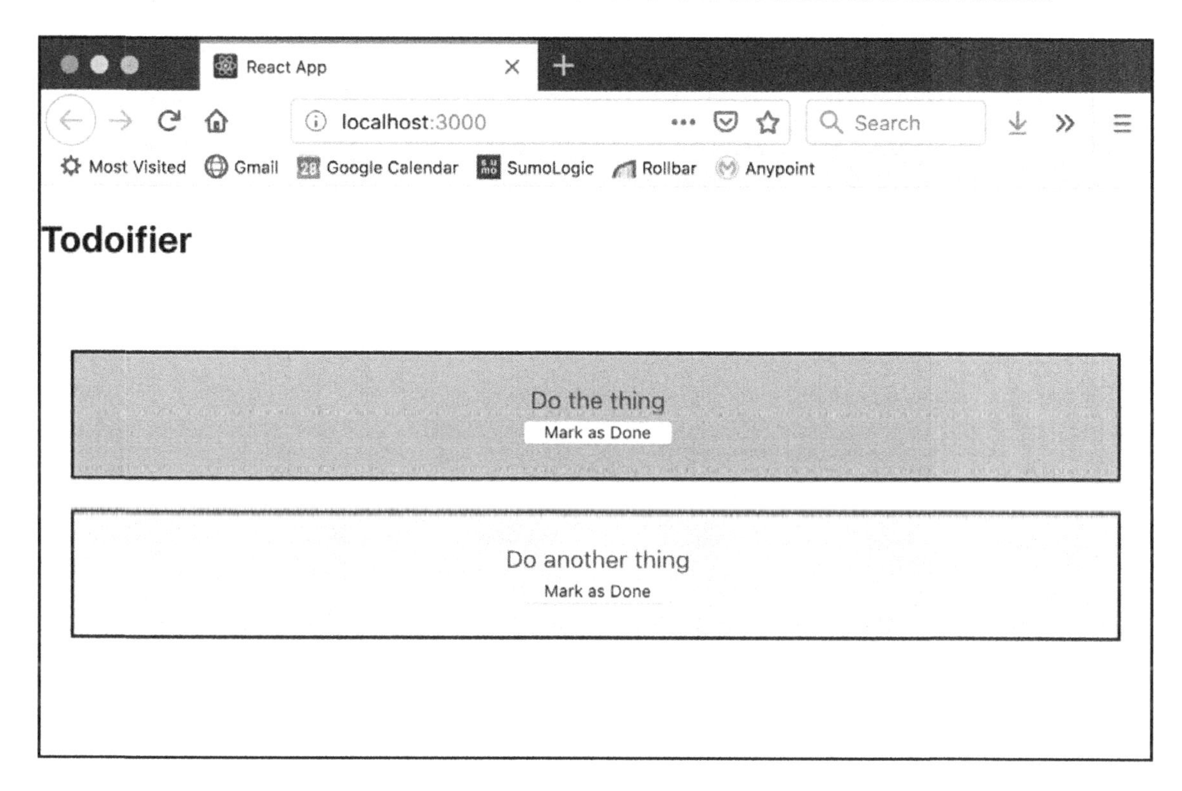

Iterating our project further

Okay, we have some state and some props in each component; we have components that can be used and reused as needed, we can see a little bit of interactivity, and we have great separation of each of our components. This brings us a little closer to writing more difficult and complex React components. More importantly, we're getting to build a larger, more complex application that will require some of the bells and whistles that we get as part of Create React App's toolset.

Building a List component

Let's take things a step further with our `Todo` components and actually create a dynamic list of components that we can add to! We'll need to start by adding a new `TodoList` that is in charge of rendering our list of `Todo` components!

We'll start by adding two new files to handle our list of Todos: `src/TodoList.js` and `src/TodoList.css`. In our `src/TodoList.js` file, we'll start off with a pretty standard React scaffold (you'll be writing something similar to this pretty often, so this will become second nature very quickly):

```
import React, { Component } from 'react';
import Todo from './Todo';
import './TodoList.css';

class TodoList extends Component {

}

export default TodoList;
```

Note that the body of our class is empty right now. We'll next need to add a `render()` function, so let's jump right to that:

```
render() {
  return (
    <div className="TodoList">
      <Todo description="Item #1" />
      <Todo description="Item #2" />
    </div>
  );
}
```

We'll also need to modify our style sheet for the `TodoList` so it's not just completely default:

```
.TodoList {
 margin: 20px;
 padding: 20px;
 border: 2px solid #00D8FF;
 background: #DDEEFF;
}
```

Adding the TodoList to our App

Right now, we just display a list of Todo items through copying and pasting the component a bunch of times, but that's not very interesting, nor is it good programming practice! Instead, let's add our List component to our App and have that be responsible for handling multiple items. We'll start off by importing our new TodoList component from the local filesystem into src/App.js:

```
import TodoList from './TodoList';
```

We'll also need to change the render() function to use the TodoList component, instead of the two Todo components directly:

```
const App = () => (
  <div className="App">
    <h2>Todoifier</h2>
    <br />
    <TodoList />
  </div>
);
```

Everything should look almost the same, except since we changed the style sheet a little bit there should be a clean little blue box around the entire list. This helps us see the distinction between each component and the parent components surrounding it.

Adding state to TodoList

We'll need some state in src/TodoList.js before we can do much else, so we'll just create an initial state that's not too exciting but gets the job done. Add a constructor to the TodoList component and give it the following body:

```
constructor(props) {
  super(props);
  this.state = { items: ['Item #1', 'Item #2'] };
}
```

Creating and using a helper render() function

Creating and initializing state but not doing anything with it doesn't help us very much, so we'll want to make sure that all of the JSX is built with the help of our state! We'll have to loop over each Todo item that is stored in our state, which we'll name this.state.items, and for each item we'll render the Todo component and, using props, pass in the description of that Todo.

We're going to use the `map` function here specifically since `map` will iterate over each item, perform a function, and then store the results as an array. JSX is expecting us to return either a single JSX element or an array of JSX elements, so this will fit our needs quite nicely. We'll also delegate this task to a new function called `renderItems()` to make sure each of our functions serves a single small purpose:

```
renderItems() {
  return this.state.items.map(description => (
    <Todo key={description} description={description} />
  ));
}
```

The only new thing here is the addition of the `key` property. This is an important part of adding multiple items in React via JSX: React has to know how to reference the item in question in some sort of unique way. If React is going to change something, delete it, or otherwise affect the DOM, it has to have something to reference the specific item by.

We're not actually guaranteeing much of anything here with the list of names; if we end up with any duplicates it will cause us issues, but this is just our naive implementation for now.

Return back to the `render()` function and we'll add a reference to our new `renderItems()` function instead of the multiple calls to `Todo`:

```
render() {
  return <div className="TodoList">{this.renderItems()}</div>;
}
```

Just to be extra sure, let's also add a third item back in our `constructor` to our initial state. If we can verify this as well, then we know we've implemented everything correctly:

```
constructor(props) {
  super(props);
  this.state = { items: ['Item #1', 'Item #2', 'Item #3'] };
}
```

There we are! Three items, all working appropriately, and all functioning entirely off of the `state`! That's a pretty good measure of progress!

Creating a new Todo component

Now that we have a good initial pass at dynamic state affecting our DOM, it's time to create a new component that will allow us to add additional `Todo` items to our `TodoList`. We'll call this, well, `NewTodo`! Create `src/NewTodo.js` and `src/NewTodo.css` to start, as per usual. Then, in `src/NewTodo.css`, give it some default style:

```
.NewTodo {
 margin: 20px;
 padding: 20px;
 border: 2px solid #00FFD8;
 background: #DDFFEE;
 text-align: center;
}
```

And then, it's time for us to build out our `NewTodo` component! We start off with our React boilerplate code that we do all the time:

```
import React, { Component } from 'react';
import './NewTodo.css';

class NewTodo extends Component {
}

export default NewTodo;
```

Next, we'll build out our `constructor()` function:

```
constructor(props) {
  super(props);
  this.state = { item: '' };
  this.handleUpdate = this.handleUpdate.bind(this);
}
```

We start off with our call to `super()`, same as always. Next, we'll set up an initial state with an `item` property that starts off blank (more on this later). We'll also need to write something to handle updates, so we'll write a `bind` statement on a `handleUpdate()` function (which we'll write next):

```
handleUpdate(event) {
  this.setState({ item: event.target.value });
}
```

So, when `handleUpdate()` is called, it is going to take a DOM event, which if we wanted to get the value of the input that is changing, we'd grab it via `event.target.value`. Finally, let's hit up our `render()` function:

```
render() {
  return (
    <div className="NewTodo">
      <input type="text" onChange={this.handleUpdate} />
        
      <button>Add</button>
    </div>
  );
}
```

Most of this code is unremarkable, but note that we have an `input` here, which is a `text` type, which reacts to every time the input's value is changed by delegating the handler to the `handleUpdate()` function we already wrote!

It's time to head back to our `TodoList`, import the `NewTodo` component, and add it near the top of our call to `render()`. At the top of `src/TodoList.js`, add the following:

```
import NewTodo from './NewTodo';
```

And then, add `NewTodo` into the `render()` function:

```
render() {
  return (
    <div className="TodoList">
      <NewTodo />
      {this.renderItems()}
    </div>
  );
}
```

Passing a function as a prop

This introduces a very interesting *chicken and egg* sort of scenario: how do we add a component to a parent from the child component? The list of `Todo` items lives in `TodoList`, and our component where we need to add new Todos is a separate component that lives inside of `TodoList`! There's no internal state for a list of Todos in `NewTodo`, so how do we make this work?

Easy! We'll create a function in TodoList, which can modify its list of components, and then pass that function into our NewTodo component. So, inside of src/TodoList.js, we'll need to add a new function called addTodo() and we will have to make sure it includes a bind() statement so that no matter where that function lives, it knows how to handle references to this. In the constructor, add our bind statement:

```
this.addTodo = this.addTodo.bind(this);
```

Let's move on to writing our addTodo() function. We'll accept a single string, which will be the description that we add. The good news is that this function is super easy to write:

```
addTodo(item) {
  this.setState({ items: [...this.state.items, item] });
}
```

We're using some new JavaScript syntax here, an array spread. This allows us to essentially take a shortcut with adding new items! Essentially, we want to add new items onto the list of items in the state, but we want to do so in a way that is non-destructive. This will make a modified copy of the item list and preserve the original. We set the list of items equal to this newly-modified array and that's it! All we have to do next is just pass this new addTodo function to NewTodo as a prop:

```
render() {
  return (
    <div className="TodoList">
      <NewTodo addTodo={this.addTodo} />
      {this.renderItems()}
    </div>
  );
}
```

Let's hop back over to src/NewTodo.js. We'll need to duplicate our function name, so we'll add an addTodo function inside of NewTodo. This is going to be called via a JavaScript event handler, so we'll need to add a bind statement for it inside of our constructor:

```
this.addTodo = this.addTodo.bind(this);
```

And, note the following for our addTodo() function body:

```
addTodo() {
  this.props.addTodo(this.state.item);
  this.setState({ item: '' });
}
```

Remember the `addTodo()` function that we passed down via props? We'll need to call that function via the props on the object and pass in the `item` property inside of our `state`. Remember, `item` is the value that is getting updated all of the time via our `onChange` event handlers! Finally, let's modify `render()` to put it all together:

```
render() {
  return (
    <div className="NewTodo">
      <input
        type="text"
        onChange={this.handleUpdate}
        value={this.state.item}
      />
        
      <button onClick={this.addTodo}>Add</button>
    </div>
  );
}
```

We need to add a new value property and set it to the current value of the `item` property from our `state`. Without doing this, we won't be able to see what is going on when we clear out the state's `item` property. Finally, we added a new `onClick` event handler that just calls out to `addTodo`, just like we prepared for!

Test it out and there we go: interactivity!

Removing items is important too

If we're adding items, we should remove them too, so we'll implement a `removeTodo()` function in the `TodoList`, and then that will get passed down into each `Todo`. This is very similar to what we did in the `NewTodo` component. We'll need to follow the same steps: add a `bind` statement, write the `removeTodo()` function, and implement calling it in the `Todo` component.

First, the bind in src/TodoList.js is as follows:

```
constructor(props) {
  super(props);
  this.state = { items: ['Item #1', 'Item #2', 'Item #3'] };

  this.addTodo = this.addTodo.bind(this);
  this.removeTodo = this.removeTodo.bind(this);
}
```

Next, we'll implement the removeTodo() function. We'll filter out any Todos that match the item we want to remove and set that as the new list of Todos:

```
removeTodo(removeItem) {
  const filteredItems = this.state.items.filter(description => {
    return description !== removeItem;
  });
  this.setState({ items: filteredItems });
}
```

The final thing we need to do is change the renderItems() call so that it passes this new function down to each Todo:

```
renderItems() {
  return this.state.items.map(description => (
    <Todo
      key={description}
      description={description}
      removeTodo={this.removeTodo}
    />
  ));
}
```

Finally, we're ready to implement this in the child component. Open up src/Todo.js, and we'll implement a duplicate-named removeTodo() function inside of the Todo component. We'll also need a bind, so we'll start this implementation in the constructor:

```
this.removeTodo = this.removeTodo.bind(this);
```

And, we'll write the removeTodo() function:

```
removeTodo() {
  this.props.removeTodo(this.state.description);
}
```

The last thing we need to do is add a call, via a `button` and an `onClick` event handler, and call the component's `removeTodo()` function:

```
render() {
 return (
 <div className={this.cssClasses()}>
 {this.state.description}
 <br />
 <button onClick={this.markAsDone}>Mark as Done</button>
 <button onClick={this.removeTodo}>Remove Me</button>
 </div>
 );
}
```

After saving and the browser refreshing, you should now be able to add and remove items on the fly! Full interactivity! Refer to the following screenshot:

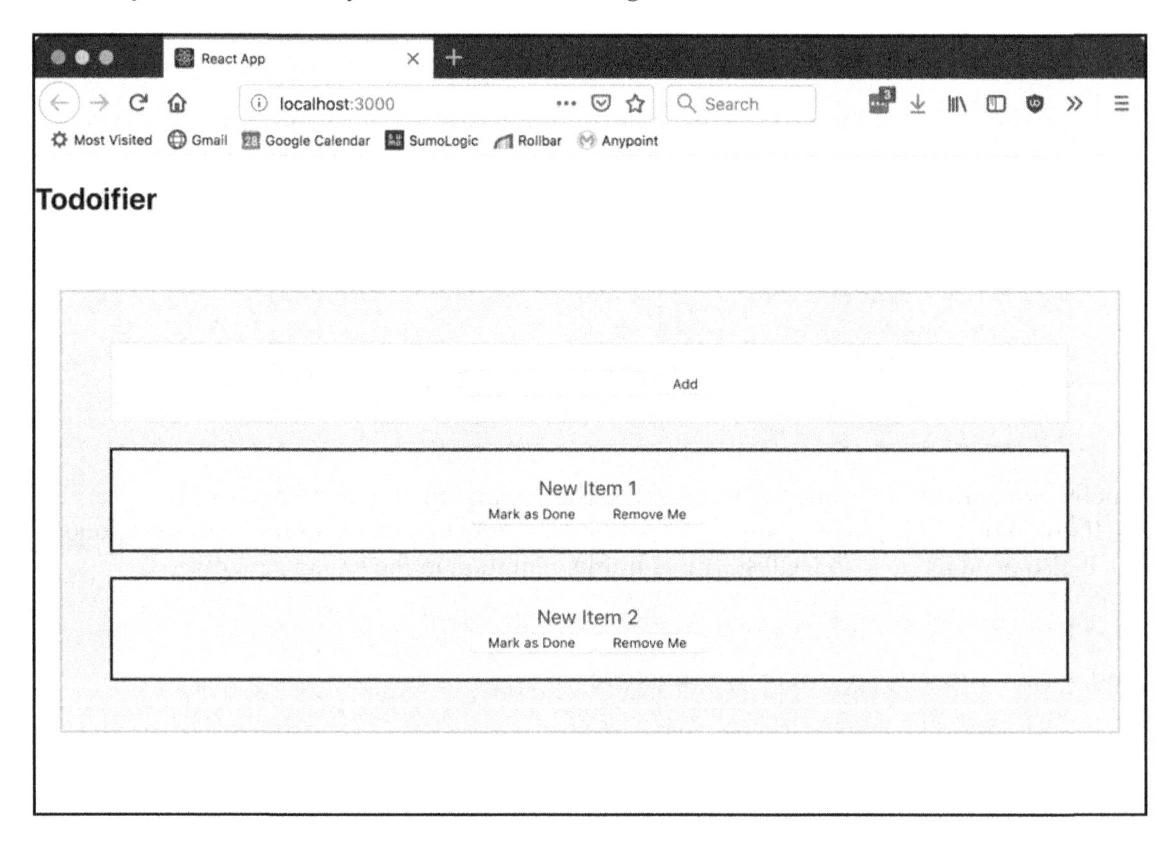

Summary

By now, you should have a strong grasp on React, how React functions, how to write good JSX and React code, and a bunch of the different gotchas and concerns you can run into. We covered all of this while still getting work done without ever having to go outside of Create React App. Now, we should have the following:

- A working Create React App project
- A more complicated application structure
- An understanding of how to affect parent structures by passing variables and functions as properties
- How to bind functions that may be called from inside event handlers

As we move on from this chapter, we'll dive more deeply into the other features of Create React App and the functionality it supports. It was important for us to have our application built and ready to go to give us room to iterate and explore the real depths of Create React App, so now that we're ready to go, we can have a lot more fun playing around with things!

3
Create React App and Babel

If you come from a background where maybe you haven't worked with JavaScript for a long time, or maybe you're new to JavaScript and Create React App is your conduit for using it, you may see a lot of syntax throughout this book and while exploring other people's projects and find that the code is hard to read without a thorough understanding of what's going on. This chapter aims to bridge that gap for people who are new to Babel and describe what it brings to the table with our Create React App project.

The other goal of this chapter is for people who are already comfortable with JavaScript, but are curious about what features Babel introduces and has turned on by default in a Create React App project, so that you can take advantage of all of the quality-of-life improvements and cleaner syntax rules in your project and really put that finishing touch on your project. The goal is to teach you production-ready code so that you're able to contribute at the highest level on your React projects.

As we work through this chapter, you can expect to get caught up on the following topics:

- Const variables
- New arrow function syntax
- Array and object destructuring
- Array and object spread operators
- React Fragments

Babel and the latest JavaScript syntax

We've been building up this application to act as our base and in the process we've introduced a lot of syntax that may not be the same JavaScript that you're used to writing! For example, we've written a few functions with this sort of syntax:

```
const foo = () => {
  doSomething();
  doSomethingElse();
}
```

The syntax here is not particularly tricky and you can probably figure out what's going on, but maybe you don't fully understand how all of that ends up as a function when all is said and done. You may be more used to writing functions in a similar pattern to the following:

```
var foo = function() {
  doSomething();
  doSomethingElse();
}
```

Or maybe something more like a function declaration without the variable, such as the following function:

```
function foo() {
  doSomething();
  doSomethingElse();
}
```

The reality is that as JavaScript progresses, there are new and more efficient methods of writing a large variety of different language constructs. Some offer helpful shortcuts, or maybe they provide a nice quality-of-life improvement for developers. Since Create React App runs on Node.js, we get some syntax improvements here and there, but generally speaking, Node integrates those new features and syntax into its standard library at a much slower pace.

Over the course of this chapter, we'll dive deeper into how to write, incorporate, and, most importantly, *understand* modern JavaScript code in our Create React App projects. We'll take a look at what features are currently supported in Create React App and learn how to take full advantage of each and every one of them!

What is Babel?

Babel is designed to bridge the gap between *the features JavaScript will have* and *the features Node.js supports right now*, and turn that resulting code into something that Node.js can understand. That means that even if Node chooses not to support something (or maybe can't support due to incompatibilities with an existing system) you're still covered!

Understanding the history

To understand why Babel is incorporated by default into Create React App projects, you need to understand a little bit of its history (similar to why it's helpful to understand the history of why Create React App was turned into a tool). Back before this handy little CLI tool, a lot of the configuration was manual, and, typically, these projects would be either built against vanilla Node.js or on browsers directly. Whatever JavaScript you wanted to do was limited to the minimum number of features that would be supported against either every version of Node that could run your code or every browser you chose to support with your application.

As a result, you ended up with basically no support for anything fun or quality of life either. Think of it like the following table:

Browser	Feature A	Feature B	Feature C	Feature D
Internet Explorer	No	Yes	No	No
Firefox	Yes	Yes	No	Yes
Chrome	Yes	Yes	Yes	No
Safari	No	Yes	Yes	Yes
What my code can support	No	Yes	No	No

Using the previous table as an example, we get to support *Feature B* in our project and absolutely nothing else! There's nothing more demoralizing than knowing you could potentially support some insanely great feature in your programming language but not being able to use it because some users would have negative or completely broken experiences.

Maybe you and your company decide that you want to pare down the number of browsers you officially support so that you can get some of these new features. Now you need to make a decision about sacrificing your user base and alienating old and new users so that you can use newer language features. Maybe it makes for a better experience for your other users and that ends up being worth the cost, but then those decisions need to be made carefully and against what percentage of your users is using what. For example, if you decided you'd only support Safari, you'd alienate every single Windows user, not just every single Internet Explorer user.

These decisions are heavy and have longstanding impacts to the health of your application. Alienating a user base at the start of your project's life could mean that it never recovers from that in the first place!

Where does Babel fit into the puzzle?

Babel comes to the rescue here by saying, *Hey, we'll give you those language features you want to use, but that not enough browsers support*. This becomes a massive relief as you start to use a larger and larger code base and run around some of the worst ways you used to have to architect larger JavaScript applications! Now if you want to use imports and new syntax and anything else, you can just do so!

Babel acts as a **transpiler**, which is a very fancy way of saying that it takes your JavaScript code that everything may not be able to be understood and turns it into JavaScript code that will be able to be understood! Babel will, based on different configurations, settings, and something called **stages**, allow you to opt in to all kinds of new syntax and language features and ensure that your code will run on most modern browsers! Granted, nothing is ever bulletproof and you will, of course, find different scenarios that aren't supported by some particular browser. You can't win them all, unfortunately!

Exploring modern JavaScript with Babel

Over the course of this section, we're going to explore the different modern JavaScript tricks and techniques that Babel allows us to use as a major part of our code. We'll take a look at the different ways that we can implement all kinds of different code and patterns, exploring the differences between the JavaScript standard ways to do certain tricks and the shorthand syntax that Babel will allow us to use. The first, especially if you haven't written any modern JavaScript in a long time, is the addition of different variable declarations, such as `const` and `let`.

The `let` variable allows us to declare a variable with very specific scoping rules. While `var` is scoped to the nearest function block and gets used as a result of that, `let` is instead scoped to the nearest block in general, and can't be used before it's declared. You also can't redeclare variables with the same name with `let`.

The `const` variable allows us to declare a constant with the same scoping rules as `let`, overall. The best practice is to use both of these far more than using `var`. In fact, I personally never use `var` if I'm working with code that I know supports const and let instead.

Now, let's move on to the first more complex thing we've run into as part of our application code: JSX!

JSX

Let's look at a very simple example of JSX code; something very similar to the code we've already written. It's easier for us to start off simple and build it up a little bit so you can see how JSX actually helps us write our code a little faster and smarter.

First off, this is just a simple `HelloWorld div` in React:

```
const HelloWorld = () => (<div>Hello World</div>);
```

Like I said, nothing particularly fancy or difficult yet. Let's take a look at the plain JavaScript version of this instead:

```
function HelloWorld() {
  return React.createElement('div', null, 'Hello World');
}
```

It does the same thing at the end of the day: it creates an `HelloWorld` React component, and then that component itself contains a single `div` with an `HelloWorld` body as the text. Where this starts to get more complicated is when you have to start including child components as well. Using our previous an `HelloWorld` component, let's expand it and make the person we're greeting configurable:

```
const HelloWorld = props => (<div>Hello {props.name}</div>);
```

The analog in regular JavaScript would be the following:

```
function HelloWorld(props) {
  return React.createElement("div", null, `Hello ${props.name}!`);
}
```

Let's open up our project and experiment with changing some of the syntax in our existing project to use the non-JSX method of creating React components and elements. Our goal is that we should get to a point where we've added a little divider in between each of the `Todo` items in our `TodoList` component. We shouldn't have to modify too much to make this work, but we're going to use the non-JSX method to build out the `Divider` component. We'll start off by creating `src/Divider.js` and `src/Divider.css`, and then we'll start off by writing `src/Divider.js` first:

```
import React from "react";
import "./Divider.css";

function Divider() {
 return React.createElement(
 "div",
 { className: "Divider" },
 React.createElement("hr")
 );
}

export default Divider;
```

There's not a whole lot extra that we're doing here; we're creating a `div` container with a class of `Divider` (you can see here why `class` isn't available for you to use in React JSX; it would not make sense, since `class` is what we use to declare classes, such as for our class-based stateful components). In our function, which doesn't take in any additional properties, we return the results of the `React.createElement()` function. `React.createElement()` takes three arguments to its call: the main element we're creating (either an HTML tag, such as `div` or `hr`, or the fully-qualified name of the function or variable, such as `Todo`), followed by an object with the properties that you're passing on to this element, and finally the array of children that should live inside that component.

Next, we'll populate our `src/Divider.css` with some fancy CSS to make our `hr` into nice gradient-based dividing lines:

```
hr {
  border: 0;
  height: 1px;
  background-image: linear-gradient(
    to right,
    rgba(0, 0, 0, 0),
    rgba(0, 0, 0, 0.8),
    rgba(0, 0, 0, 0)
  );
}
```

Next, go into `src/TodoList.js`, where we'll `import` our new `Divider` and modify a little bit of code to include the new divider. First, we'll start off with `import` at the top:

```
import Divider from "./Divider";
```

Then we'll actually place the `Divider` inside of the code. We'll need to go down to the `renderItems()` function and change the body to wrap `Todo` inside of a `div` container (we can get around this by using React Fragments, but we'll talk about this more a little bit later), and then include the `Divider` component at the bottom of that. Also, note that for each of the key properties in the following JSX code, we're prefixing the "description" with a little description of the component we're building to avoid collisions:

```
  renderItems() {
    return this.state.items.map(description => (
      <div key={"div-" + description}>
        <Todo
          key={description}
          description={description}
          removeTodo={this.removeTodo}
        />
        <Divider key={"divide-" + description}/>
      </div>
    ));
  }
```

Save and reload, and we should have some new dividers breaking up our `Todo` items:

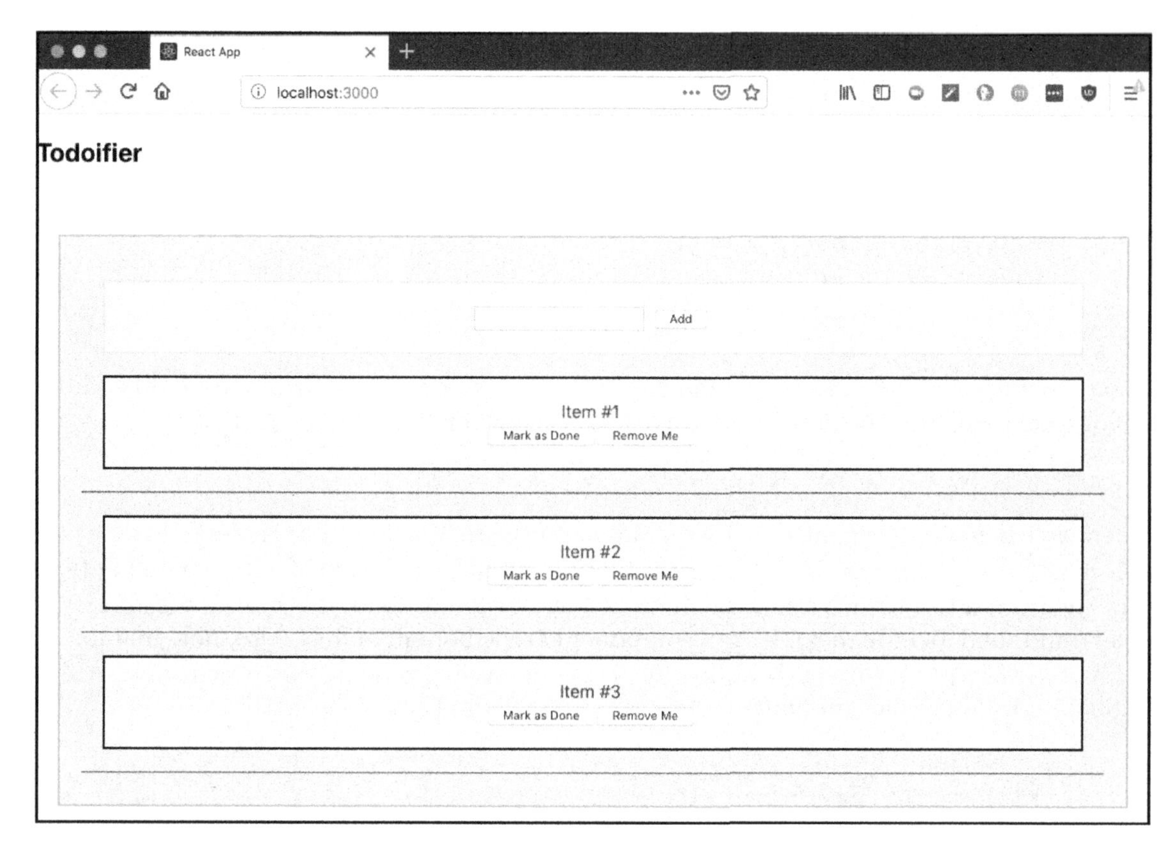

And there we are, a new `Divider` written entirely in vanilla JavaScript!

The next code snippet is just provided as an example of what a full, more complicated function would look like written without any JSX. You don't actually need to do any of this work!

Just for fun, let's take a look at what our two `render()` function calls in `TodoList` would look like without JSX:

```
renderItems() {
  return this.state.items.map(description =>
    React.createElement("div", { key: "div-" + description }, [
      React.createElement(Todo, {
        key: description,
        description: description,
```

```
          removeTodo: this.removeTodo
        }),
        React.createElement(Divider, { key: "divider-" + description })
      ])
    );
  }
  render() {
    return React.createElement("div", { className: "TodoList" }, [
      React.createElement(NewTodo, { addTodo: this.addTodo }),
      this.renderItems()
    ]);
  }
```

Everything will still function exactly the same, so if this was something you wanted to pursue and you preferred this syntax to JSX, that remains an option for you.

Function syntax

Let's also spend a little bit of time talking about the different ways to write functions that we can take advantage of when using Babel paired with Create React App. In the code we wrote previously, we already talked a bit about this and showed a few examples of alternate function syntax, but we're going to dive more deeply into everything now.

Ultimately, there are a few standard ways in JavaScript, without any frills, to declare a function. We can either choose the method of declaring a function with the `function` keyword, or we could declare it as a variable. Let's look at a few examples:

```
function sayHello(name) {
  console.log(`Hello ${name}!`);
}
```

We could also write this, without using any frills from Babel, via the following code:

```
var sayHello = function(name) {
  console.log(`Hello ${name}!`);
}
```

And the way that we'd invoke that function after having built it is just simply via the following:

```
sayHello('Mason');
```

So now, think back to some of the other functions that we've written over the previous two chapters. We've frequently defined functions using a `const` statement, which would turn the `function` we've written previously into the following instead:

```
const sayHello = name => {
 console.log(`Hello ${name}!`);
};
```

While this is practically identical to the variable method of declaring functions in old JavaScript, there's a minor difference in terms of the syntax that's worth pointing out, and that's in the way that the function signature is declared in the code.

Previously, after our variable declaration, we'd write the function and then parentheses with the arguments in it. In modern JavaScript, we can use something called **arrow functions**. Arrow functions are a shorthand syntax shortcut with an extra benefit in terms of how `this` gets bound. Specifically, the context of `this` when the function is declared is the context of `this` when the function is declared. Instead of the function taking and defining its own context for `this`, it instead uses `this` in the current scope.

The rules for declaring arrow functions are pretty simple:

- If you have no arguments, you must declare the function with parentheses and then the fat arrow (=>):

  ```
  const foo = () => { return "Hi!"; }
  ```

- If you have one argument, you can optionally include the parentheses:

  ```
  const foo = name => { return `Hi ${name}!` };
  ```

- If you have two or more arguments, you must include the parentheses:

  ```
  const foo = (greeting, name) => { return `${greeting} ${name}!`; }
  ```

- If you're returning something as a single-line function, you don't need to use curly brackets or a `return` statement:

  ```
  const foo = (greeting, name) => `${greeting} ${name}`;
  ```

- If you're returning something as a multi-line function, you must use curly brackets and a `return` statement:

  ```
  const foo = (greeting, name) => {
      const message = greeting + " " + name + "!";
      return message;
  };
  ```

Destructuring

Modern JavaScript also gives us better access to destructuring. Destructuring is a way of matching the patterns in data structures (for example, in arrays or objects) and being able to turn those into individual variables in function arguments or in variable declarations. Let's mess around with a few different examples to get a good feel for how destructuring works and how we can better take advantage of it. Open up `src/App.js`, where we'll use destructuring a few times. Before we make our change, the `App` function should look like the following code:

```
const App = () => (
  <div className="App">
    <h2>Todoifier</h2>
    <br />
    <TodoList />
  </div>
);
```

Nothing exciting yet, so let's make this code exciting! We'll start off by allowing you to rename your app, since maybe you don't feel that `Todoifier` is a great name for an app! We'll start off by adding a simple data structure above our code:

```
const details = {
  header: "Todoifier",
  headerColor: "red"
};
```

Next, we'll destructure this data structure into a single variable name. We'll add the following line right after we declare our `details` data structure:

```
const { header } = details;
```

What we're doing here is rewriting the structure of the data structure we created in the `details` variable and then saying that we want it to take the value in the `header` key of the `details` variable and ignore everything else, and then throw it into the `header` variable. The end result is that we should expect to see `Todoifier` in the `header` variable. Just to make sure, let's throw a `console.log` statement and verify the results:

```
console.log("appName is " + appName);
```

We should see it show up in our JavaScript console in the browser if all went well:

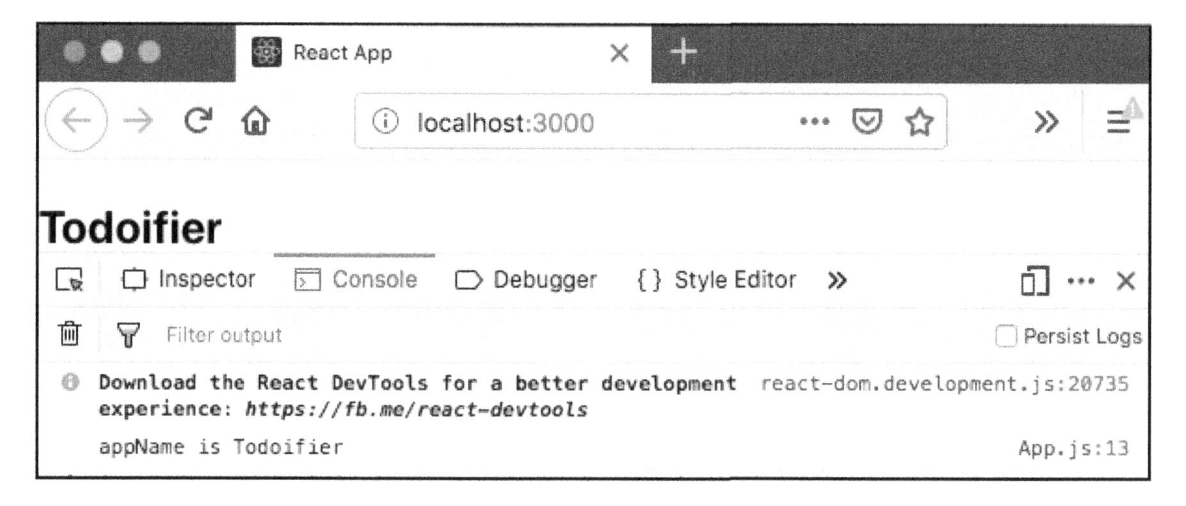

There we are! Now that we know this works, let's hop back over to the `App` component and add in a reference to the `header` variable:

```
const App = () => (
  <div className="App">
    <h2>{appName}</h2>
    <br />
    <TodoList />
  </div>
);
```

When our page refreshes, we should see whatever value you threw in the `header` value in the `details` variable! Let's make it a little cleaner and a little bit closer to what you'd normally expect to see in production code, because right now the code we've written is a bit redundant. Delete the reference to `appName` and the `console.log` statement and we'll write a new function to use in our component:

```
const headerDisplay = ({ header: title, headerColor: color }) => (
  <h2 style={{ color: color }}>{title}</h2>
);
```

We're actually using a few separate tricks here! We're using the new function declaration syntax and simple function `return` syntax, and we're using destructuring to make our code super simple and clean! We destructure a passed-in argument to pull the `title` and `headerColor` out and store those in the title and `color` variables, respectively!

We then pass those into the `h2` tag to set the CSS `color` style and the displayed `title` of the application! The final step is that we need to hook up this component to use the new `header` function we just defined:

```
const App = () => (
  <div className="App">
    {headerDisplay(details)}
    <br />
    <TodoList />
  </div>
);
```

And there we are! With this code in place, we should see a red header with the name **Todoifier**! Let's take a look:

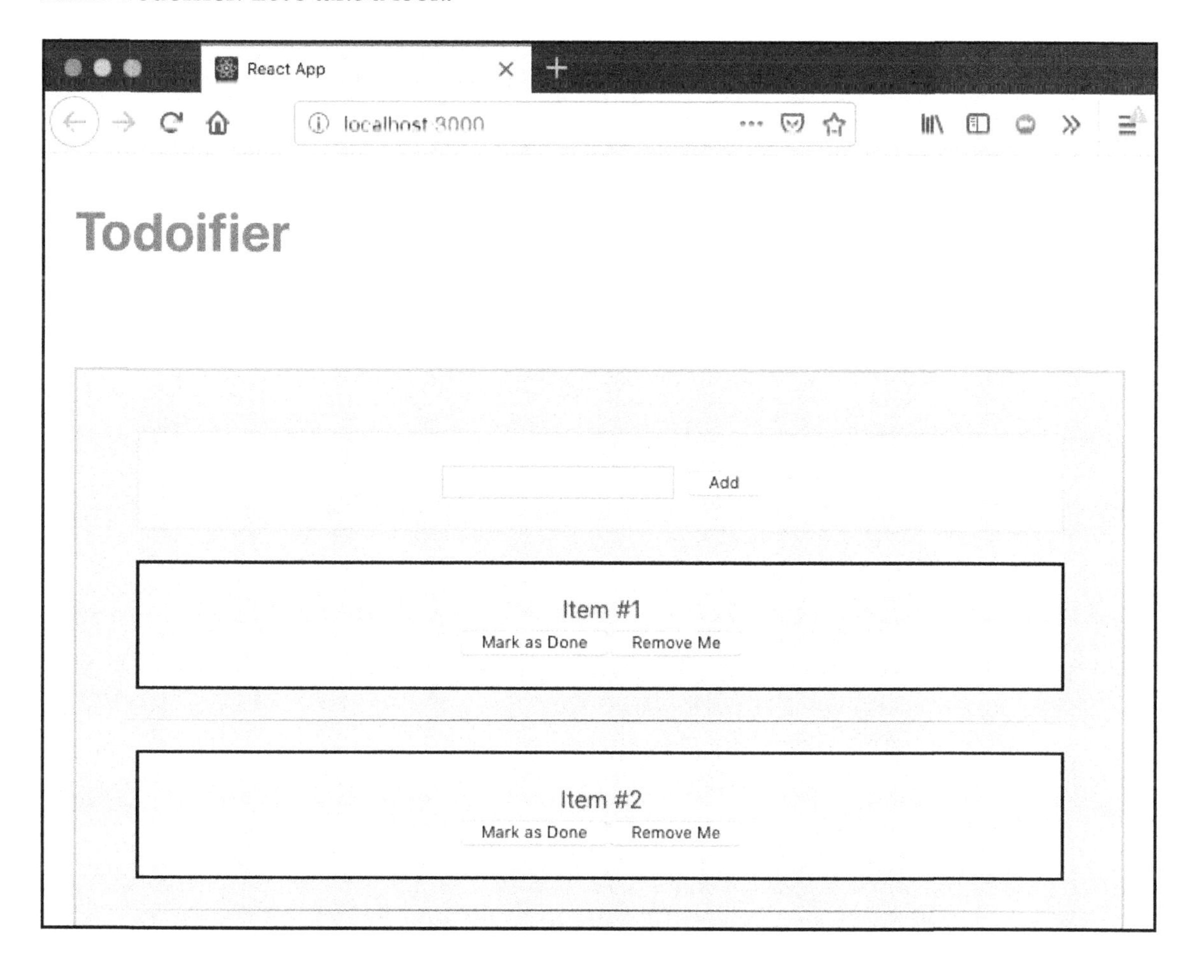

We can actually destructure arrays as well! For example, let's say we have a few unique options we want to start off our list with. We can capture those as named variables through array-destructuring, and we can also take advantage of some other syntax tricks we'll learn later, such as array spreads! Let's take a look at `src/TodoList.js` and change our constructor to use array-destructuring:

```
const [item1, item2, ...rest] = [
  "Write some code",
  "Change the world",
  "Take a nap",
  "Eat a cookie"
];
this.state = {
  items: [item1, item2, rest.join(" and ")]
};
```

Array-destructuring is just based on position; the only new trick here is that after matching `item1` and `item2`, we're just going to throw the remainder of the array onto a variable called `rest`, which we'll join with some spaces and the word `"and"`. Let's see the result:

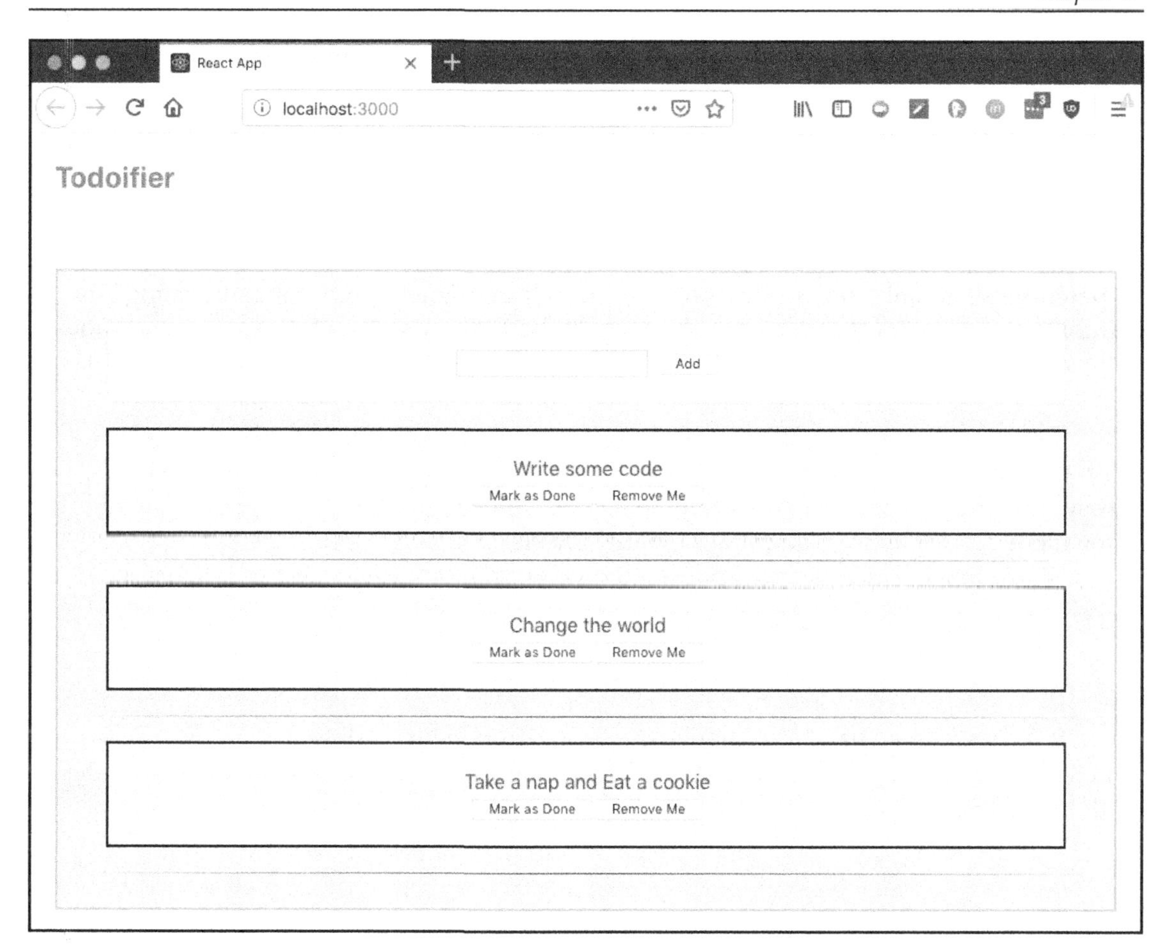

Optional arguments

Setting optional arguments for functions is thankfully a pretty simple endeavor! If you want to make a `function` argument optional, all you need to do is add an equals sign after the name of the parameter and give it a default value. For example, let's revisit the `sayHello` function we wrote a little bit earlier in this chapter:

```
const sayHello = name => {
  console.log(`Hello ${name}!`);
};
```

Now, let's modify that so that if someone doesn't specify a `name`, the function call will not just fail out or throw an error for the developer:

```
const sayHello = (name = "Unknown") => {
  console.log(`Hello ${name}!`);
};
```

Note that since we're using an optional variable for the argument list, we need to enclose it in parentheses again! Now, if someone were to call that function without specifying any parameters, we'd expect to see in our console **Hello Unknown!**, something similar to the following:

```
sayHello();
```

With that, let's write this into our previous `headerDisplay` function. It will be a little messy, sure, but it's great to know how to use this effectively, since it's a great way to implement defensive programming in your projects:

```
const headerDisplay = ({
  header: title = "Todo List",
  headerColor: color = "blue"
}) => <h2 style={{ color: color }}>{title}</h2>;
```

Now, if we were to go back and change our App component's call to the `header()` function to just pass in a blank object, we would expect the header to instead say `TodoList` with a blue header:

```
const App = () => (
  <div className="App">
    {headerDisplay({})}
    <br />
    <TodoList />
  </div>
);
```

Let's see the results before we revert the change to our `header` function and change it back into passing in the `details` variable:

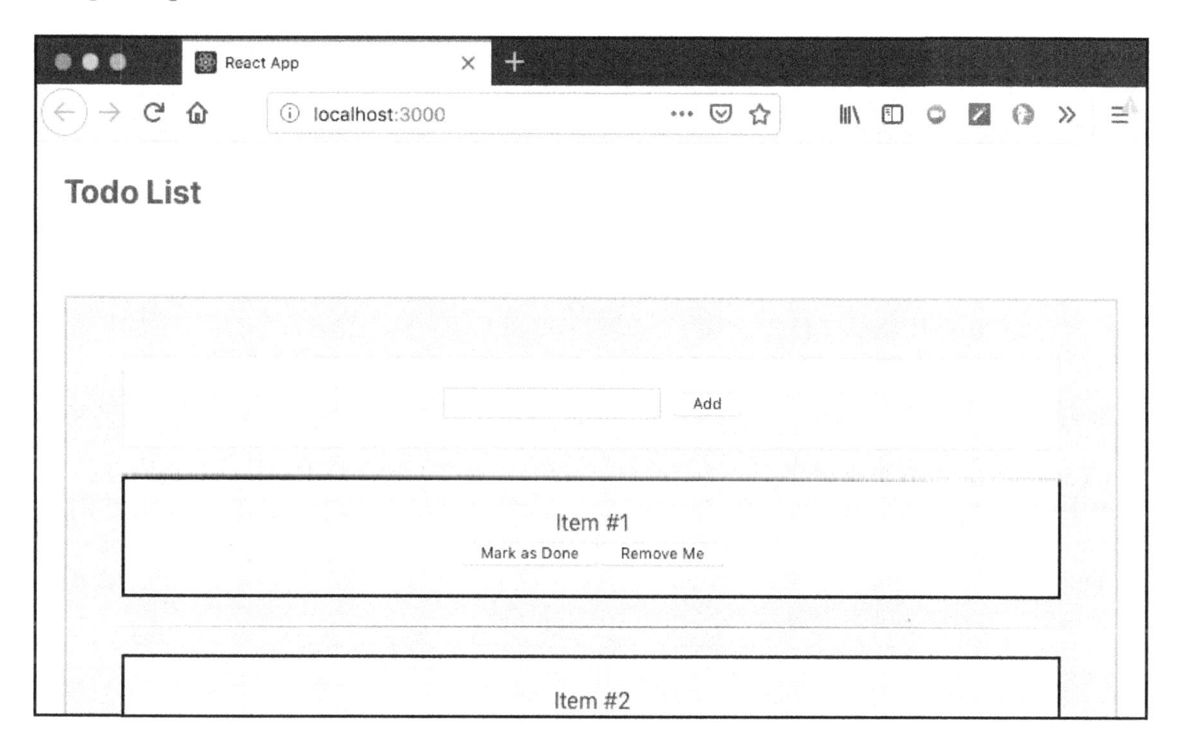

The spread operator

Remember a little bit earlier in the chapter, when we wrote an ellipse and then a variable name? Any time you do that, you're telling JavaScript to stuff the rest of the unmatched stuff into here and join it to the current data structure:

```
const [item1, item2, ...rest] = [
  "Write some code",
  "Change the world",
  "Take a nap",
  "Eat a cookie"
];
```

This line of code tells JavaScript that the item in the first spot goes into the `item1` variable, the item in the second spot goes into the `item2` variable, and then everything else after that goes into the `rest` variable. We can take advantage of this as well when we want to add items onto an array in a non-destructive way. Remember the `addTodo()` function that lives in `src/TodoList.js`? Let's take a look at that in greater detail to see how we can use array spreads elsewhere:

```
addTodo(item) {
  this.setState({ items: [...this.state.items, item] });
}
```

This line of code is telling JavaScript to set the `items` key in the component's `state` to be equal to the current value of `this.state.items`, and then concatenate `item` onto the end of that list. The code is identical to this:

```
this.setState({ items: this.state.items.concat(item) });
```

You can also do this with objects in JavaScript code with Babel's most recent update in Create React App, which is great for `state` modification, since `state` modification is just changing objects around! Let's head back to `src/App.js` and write a sample bit of code that also sets a background color for our `header`. We'll start off with our object spread and set a new variable called `moreDetails`:

```
const moreDetails = {
  ...details,
  header: "Best Todoifier",
  background: "black"
};
```

We're just taking the `details` data structure, and then on top of that, we're either adding new keys or replacing values for existing keys. Next, we'll need to modify the `headerDisplay` function to be able to work with a background color being passed in:

```
const headerDisplay = ({
  header: title = "Todo List",
  headerColor: color = "blue",
  background: background = "none"
}) => <h2 style={{ color: color, background: background }}>{title}</h2>;
```

The final step of this is to change the call in the `App` component to pass in `moreDetails` to the `header` instead of `details` or a blank object:

```
const App = () => (
  <div className="App">
    {headerDisplay(moreDetails)}
```

```
      <br />
      <TodoList />
    </div>
  );
```

After you save and reload, you should see the following:

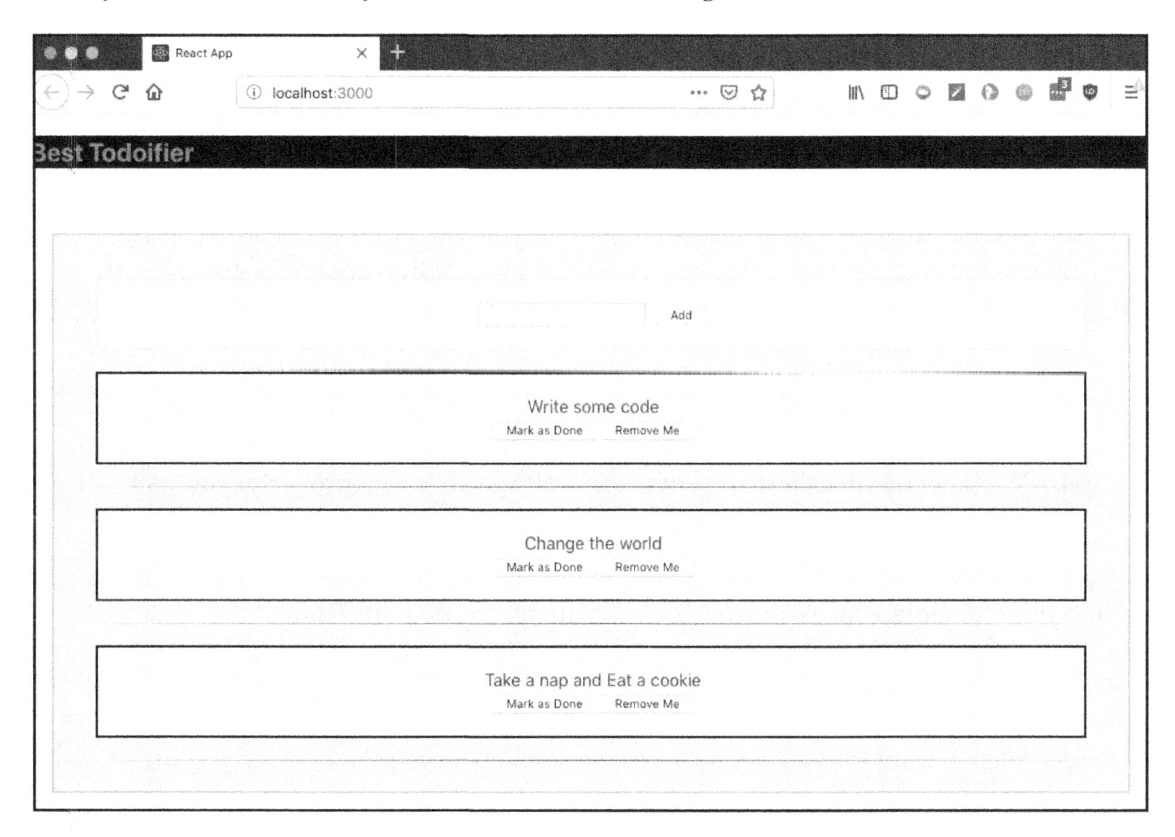

The line of code for the `Object` spread is the equivalent of us writing the following:

```
const moreDetails = Object.assign({}, details, {
  header: "Best Todoifier",
  background: "black"
});
```

It's just a little more concise and easier to read, so it's great that the Create React App team and the Babel team made this supported in the most recent version!

React Fragments

The final thing we're going to talk about in this chapter is the new support for React Fragments! React Fragments are a brand-new, but important, feature. Previously, if you wanted to include multiple components at the same level, you *always* had to have a root component, even for things such as multiple table rows, which never really made sense; you'd have to nest `<td>` tags inside of `<div>`, which is just weird.

It ends up with you having to choose between writing what's technically invalid HTML or writing compliant React code, which tends to just end up as awkward or bad code to get around the limitation. Now, instead, we can write code encased in special Fragment tags (`<Fragment>` and `</Fragment>`) to denote the start and end of a fragment, respectively. We can reference these as `<React.Fragment>`, `<Fragment>` (if we choose to `import Fragment` where we `import Component`, such as in the following line of code), or as `<>` for a shortcut:

```
import React, { Fragment, Component } from "react";
```

A quick warning about using the shortcut syntax of `<>` and `</>`: if you're using Fragments inside of code that's building a list of Fragments, you can't use the shortcut syntax and still specify a `key` property; you will have to use either `React.Fragment` or `Fragment`.

If we go back to `src/TodoList.js`, in our `renderItems()` function, we can see the perfect place to replace an extraneous `<div>` with a `Fragment` instead:

```
renderItems() {
return this.state.items.map(description => (
<Fragment key={"item-" + description}>
 <Todo
  key={description}
  description={description}
  removeTodo={this.removeTodo}
 />
<Divider key={"divide-" + description} />
 </Fragment>
));
}
```

At the top of the function, where we `import Component` as a named `import` from `React`, we'll also need to include `Fragment`, similar to the line of code a little bit higher up in this section.

The end result is otherwise identical; the major difference is that instead of placing each of the Todos and Dividers inside of extra `div` for no reason, they can all sit next to each other in the DOM tree and keep your code significantly cleaner, especially in the case of working with HTML tables, where introducing an extra `div` will actually just break your code!

A quick recap

Before we end this chapter, let's look at the final state of all of the code that we've written. Our `src/TodoList.js` has expanded and includes a lot of new tricks:

```
import React, { Fragment, Component } from "react";
import Todo from "./Todo";
import "./TodoList.css";

import NewTodo from "./NewTodo";
import Divider from "./Divider";

class TodoList extends Component {
  constructor(props) {
    super(props);
    const [item1, item2, ...rest] = [
      "Write some code",
      "Change the world",
      "Take a nap",
      "Eat a cookie"
    ];
    this.state = {
      items: [item1, item2, rest.join(" and ")]
    };

    this.addTodo = this.addTodo.bind(this);
    this.removeTodo = this.removeTodo.bind(this);
  }
  addTodo(item) {
    this.setState({ items: [...this.state.items, item] });
  }
  removeTodo(removeItem) {
    const filteredItems = this.state.items.filter(description => {
      return description !== removeItem;
    });
    this.setState({ items: filteredItems });
  }
  renderItems() {
    return this.state.items.map(description => (
      <Fragment key={"item-" + description}>
```

```
          <Todo
            key={description}
            description={description}
            removeTodo={this.removeTodo}
          />
          <Divider key={"divide-" + description} />
        </Fragment>
      ));
    }
    render() {
      return (
        <div className="TodoList">
          <NewTodo addTodo={this.addTodo} />
          {this.renderItems()}
        </div>
      );
    }
  }

  export default TodoList;
```

Our `src/App.js` component has expanded significantly as well:

```
import React from "react";
import "./App.css";

import TodoList from "./TodoList";

const details = {
 header: "Todoifier",
 headerColor: "red"
};

const moreDetails = {
 ...details,
 header: "Best Todoifier",
 background: "black"
};

const App = () => (
 <div className="App">
 {header(moreDetails)}
 <br />
 <TodoList />
 </div>
);

const header = ({
```

```
  header: title = "Todo List",
  headerColor: color = "blue",
  background: background = "none"
 }) => <h2 style={{ color: color, background: background }}>{title}</h2>;

 export default App;
```

Summary

We covered a lot, but were pretty productive! We talked a lot about how to take full advantage of the better and cleaner syntax that Babel offers us in a Create React App 2 project!

Even this is really just scratching the surface of what you can do in modern JavaScript, but it covers a lot of the common patterns and tricks that you'll see throughout this book. We hope this guide will give you everything you need to be able to execute projects and to understand and contribute at the highest levels!

We'll be exploring a lot of these code techniques in future chapters, so make sure you have a firm grasp of everything we discussed in this chapter before you forge ahead!

4
Keep Your App Healthy with Tests and Jest

An important part of any application developer's life is making sure that their application runs properly the first time, every time. That can be a difficult thing to do as applications get more complicated; what might have previously required just a few minutes and a single line of code to clean up or fix might instead start taking hours, days, or even weeks (or longer) to try to fix! In addition, if you're trying to build up your application and make it work cleanly and effectively.

In this chapter, we will cover the following topics:

- The history of testing React applications
- Different ways to run React tests
- A brief introduction to Jest
- A brief introduction to the test watcher
- How to write tests

The why and when of testing

You might be wondering why we've started tackling our tests so late in our application. Generally speaking, when you're just starting out in your projects, you might wait a little bit to see how your application shakes out before you start verifying its behavior with tests. That being said, we're now also at a really good point to start shoring up our project and make it something that we can deploy to production with confidence!

The history of testing React

Again, it's great to understand the history of the toolset to understand why certain features or libraries are being used. When people were just getting started with React, ideas and standards around testing were absolutely all over the place. Some people used weird combinations of libraries that had all sorts of names, such as night-something, mocha, or some other random framework. You had to figure out mocking libraries, test harnesses, and user interface test frameworks.

It was absolutely *exhausting*, and inevitably any framework and setup you were using would either fall out of favor or fall out of date and you'd have to turn around and start learning a new one every few weeks! Even worse, if you asked a ton of different people what their particular test setup was, you'd get at least that many different answers!

About Jest

Jest was the React team's answer to the constant question of *what test harness should we use for our React application?* You'd always get a different answer depending on who you asked, and sometimes you'd have to use multiple harnesses just to get features you wanted, which led to a ton of bloat and developer confusion about which one was the correct one to use at any given time!

Analyzing the structure of Jest tests

The best place for us to get started is to take a look at the default standard test that comes with any new Create React App project, and that is the test for our `App` component, located at `src/App.test.js`:

```
import React from 'react';
import ReactDOM from 'react-dom';
import App from './App';

it('renders without crashing', () => {
  const div = document.createElement('div');
  ReactDOM.render(<App />, div);
  ReactDOM.unmountComponentAtNode(div);
});
```

Well, this isn't a particularly *exciting* test by any stretch of the imagination. As the name implies, this test just verifies that the `App` component can be rendered on the page without any major hiccups or errors. This test might seem kind of superfluous, but it actually serves an incredibly important purpose: it remains as a sanity check for your application!

Think about it: if your main application or component couldn't render without any other more complicated checks, then your project is very, very broken! It helps us check whether we're accidentally excluding things or introducing significantly breaking changes to our project in a way that keeps us all sane! Let's also verify that this actually does work the way we expect even with our changes right now:

```
$ yarn test
```

When we run this, we should expect to see some output in our console window that tells us a little more about what tests were run, what tests passed, what failed, and other metadata about our test run as well:

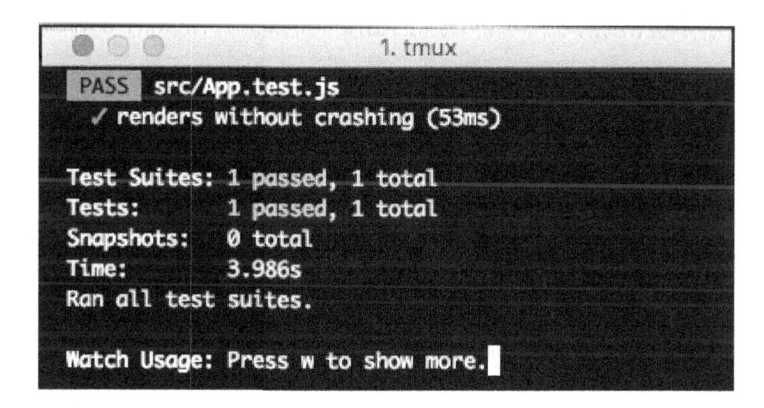

Just like that, clean and working tests! Now, that by itself is really cool, but let's take a few minutes to analyze the previous output window!

Exploring the test output

Right now, if we just look at the previous output without any context, it may not make a ton of sense! Let's start off by taking a look at the first line after the test, which talks about our **Test Suites**:

```
Test Suites: 1 passed, 1 total
```

Jest allows us to run and organize our tests in a number of different and helpful ways! For example, our tests can be run by suites; suites being larger groupings of tests. We'll explore this line of output a little further later on when we have more than a single test, but right now we only have one test suite, and thus we've only run a single test suite:

```
Tests: 1 passed, 1 total
```

We ran a single test, and that single test passed! This allows us to also keep track of what tests were run as our application code changed; we may not need to run every single test in every single suite across the board when we make minor changes! Instead, we can focus on the tests that would be affected by whatever the change was, so you may see this as being less than the total number of tests in your suites:

```
Snapshots: 0 total
```

Snapshots are a different feature entirely with Jest. Snapshots are a way to tell Jest that *given input X, the rendered component should look exactly like this*. We'll explore this in greater detail later! The following line indicates how long our tests took to run:

```
Time: 3.986s
```

This is important to note, as sometimes you might introduce some code to your application that makes your application incredibly slow! This can help you catch those sneaky performance-ruining bits of code in your application. Your tests will essentially be your early-warning system against poorly-performing algorithms! We will get the following output:

```
Ran all test suites.
Watch Usage: Press w to show more.
```

Finally, we get some output that tells us a little bit about what tests ran and what else we can do. We can also hit *w* here to get more options about what we can do with our test runner and watcher:

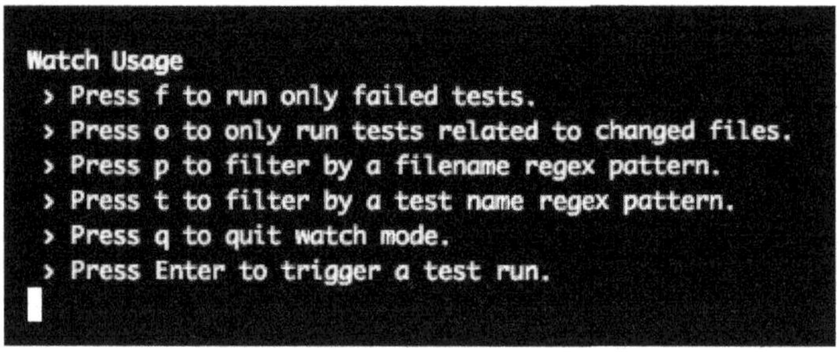

```
Watch Usage
 › Press f to run only failed tests.
 › Press o to only run tests related to changed files.
 › Press p to filter by a filename regex pattern.
 › Press t to filter by a test name regex pattern.
 › Press q to quit watch mode.
 › Press Enter to trigger a test run.
```

A development test workflow with the F key

When we hit *w*, we get a new list of commands that we can run to continue with our test suite and do more for it. We've already explored these options a little bit, but it's worth reiterating the work that we can (and should) do during development and talk a little bit about *when* to use these tests as well!

The first major one is the following:

```
Press f to run only failed tests
```

We'll use this one *a lot*. Often when you're developing complex applications you might introduce changes that break your test suite, or you might be going with more of a test-driven development approach, in which case you'll be working with broken tests and then fixing things in your application or in your tests until the tests pass again! If that's the case, you'll be using this command a lot, so get comfortable with it early! If we try to run this now without any failed tests, we'll get the following output:

```
No failed test found.
Press `f` to quit "only failed tests" mode.

Watch Usage: Press w to show more.
```

This makes sense. We had no failed tests, so of course it wouldn't find any and thus wouldn't run any tests. We can make this work for us, though, by introducing a failing test intentionally and then running our full test suite, followed by just the failed tests! We can simulate this very quickly by returning back to `src/App.js` and commenting out the `export` statement at the bottom of the code:

```
// export default App;
```

Now if you restart your tests, you will get one failing test! We should be able to hit *F* and it will rerun the single failing test (and we can repeat this process over and over, as well). Now if we uncomment that line and save the file, if we rerun our test suite (either automatically or manually using *F*), we should be back to a fully-working test suite!

There's another reason to get comfortable with rerunning failed tests: you should get comfortable with the idea of writing tests that intentionally fail until you make the test pass, or passes unless you comment or intentionally break the code! If you make code changes that should break your tests but the test still passes, that means your tests aren't actually testing the behavior of your application correctly!

It's time to add some new tests!

We have a pretty good understanding of our initial test, but there's so much more we can learn by writing new tests! We'll start off by testing the absolute simplest component that we've written so far: our `Todo` component! You'll notice a pattern with how we have to name our tests to have Jest pick them up appropriately: we'll create a test for our `Todo` component (in `src/Todo.js`) as `src/Todo.test.js`! We'll almost always want to start off our tests by mimicking the structure in `App.test.js`, so we'll start off by doing almost the same things:

```
import React from "react";
import ReactDOM from "react-dom";
import Todo from "./Todo";

it("renders without crashing", () => {
 const div = document.createElement("div");
 ReactDOM.render(<Todo />, div);
 ReactDOM.unmountComponentAtNode(div);
});
```

After rerunning our **Test Suite** (you may have to exit out of the test watcher with *Q* and rerun `yarn test`), you should get the following output:

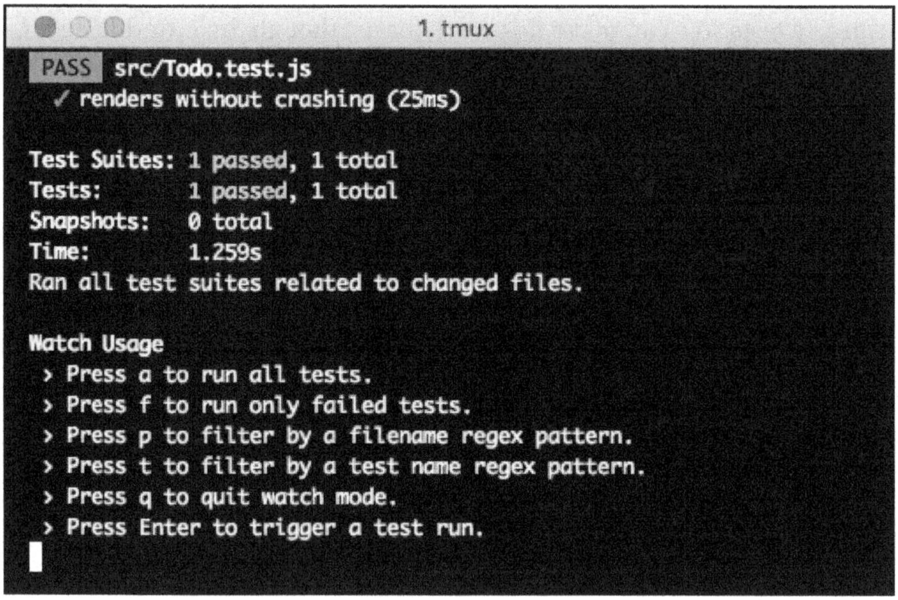

```
1. tmux
PASS src/Todo.test.js
  ✓ renders without crashing (25ms)

Test Suites: 1 passed, 1 total
Tests:       1 passed, 1 total
Snapshots:   0 total
Time:        1.259s
Ran all test suites related to changed files.

Watch Usage
 › Press a to run all tests.
 › Press f to run only failed tests.
 › Press p to filter by a filename regex pattern.
 › Press t to filter by a test name regex pattern.
 › Press q to quit watch mode.
 › Press Enter to trigger a test run.
```

So it ran our `src/Todo.test.js` test that we just added, and it's a new test suite as well! Let's expand out our tests since right now they're not really doing anything. To do that, however, we'll need to add a few more libraries to our test suite! We'll want to add `enzyme` (for shallow rendering); `enzyme` is a React v16.x adapter, and React's test `renderer` to our application. We can do so with one quick `yarn` command:

```
$ yarn add --dev react-test-renderer enzyme enzyme enzyme-adapter-react-16
```

`enzyme` adds a lot to our test suite and makes it that much easier to work with, so it's honestly worth it to include `enzyme` as a baseline to our test suite! In fact, it's so helpful that it's included on some of the default React/Jest test documentation! Now, just including these by themselves won't do everything we need, so we'll also need to create a test setup file to initialize Enzyme. Create `src/setupTests.js` and give it the following body:

```
// setup file
import { configure } from 'enzyme';
import Adapter from 'enzyme-adapter-react-16';

configure({ adapter: new Adapter() });
```

Having done that, we can start tackling some real test code! We'll need to open up `src/Todo.test.js`, where we can add some code at the top which will give us the ability to take advantage of the `enzyme` shallow `renderer`! We'll also need `react-test-renderer` of the `renderer()` function, since we'll use that to create snapshots:

```
import React from "react";
import ReactDOM from "react-dom";
import { shallow } from "enzyme";
import renderer from "react-test-renderer";

import Todo from "./Todo";
```

Now we have everything we need to begin writing our tests. Before we start writing our tests, I generally begin by throwing all of our tests into a big `describe` function, so let's start off there by moving the test that we already wrote inside of our `describe` block:

```
describe(Todo, () => {
  it("renders without crashing", () => {
    const div = document.createElement("div");
    ReactDOM.render(<Todo />, div);
    ReactDOM.unmountComponentAtNode(div);
  });
});
```

Rerun the tests and we should be back to green and two suites and two tests:

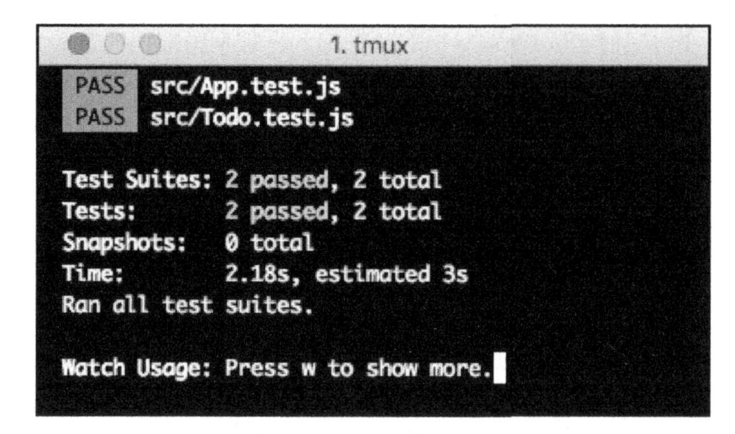

Describe is a way of blocking together related tests, whether by functionality, concept, or otherwise. You have a few ways to declare a describe block. You can either use a string to specify the name of a test, or you can use a valid `Class` or `Component` name.

Now, if we want to start making our tests a little more complicated, we'll also need to do some basic setup stuff, since if you remember from our `Todo` component, we have a few functions that need to get passed down into our child component. Let's take a look at the default `props` of our `Todo`:

```
this.state = {
  done: false
};
```

And the function body of the `removeTodo` prop:

```
removeTodo() {
  this.props.removeTodo(this.props.description);
}
```

Description is easy; that's just a string that we need to pass in. `removeTodo(...)`, on the other hand, is more complicated. It's a function that doesn't live as part of this component; instead, it lives inside of the parent and is passed in! So, how do we deal with that?

Simple, we can *mock* a function with Jest! Mocking a function basically makes a fake function that keeps track of when it's called. We'll also need to perform a **shallow render** of our component to verify how the component appears in the DOM overall. We'll talk a little more about this in a minute, but for right now add the following at the top of the describe block:

```
const description = "New Todo";
const mockRemoveTodo = jest.fn();
const component = shallow(
  <Todo description={description} removeTodo={mockRemoveTodo} />
);
```

As you can see from the previous example, `jest.fn()` allows us to create a mocked function. Mocking a function, as mentioned previously, doesn't do anything in particular. It pretends to be a function, sees who is trying to use that function, and also keeps track of things, such as fake arguments or sets up fake return values for the function. This is good if we want to verify that the `removeTodo` in our `props` actually does anything at all but we don't care that it performs a specific behavior.

Writing a generic snapshot test

Talking about writing tests is one thing, but let's actually start implementing our tests. I typically approach test-writing in the following way:

- Write a generic snapshot test
- Write some subcomponent-specific tests
- Check content
- Check interactions

Snapshot tests can be used to verify initial state renders and renders after specific conditions are met. This works by grabbing a representation of your component, storing that, and then using it for future tests. This can be tricky when you have components that are changing constantly, but can be incredibly handy when your components are stable and shouldn't be getting modified often. Let's write our `snapshot` test:

```
it("renders and matches our snapshot", () => {
  const component = renderer.create(<Todo description="Yo" />);
  const tree = component.toJSON();
  expect(tree).toMatchSnapshot();
});
```

Remember the `renderer` we had to `import` from `react-test-renderer`? This is where we use it! We create a `Todo` component via JSX and pass that into the `renderer.create()` function. We then grab the component structure, transform it into JSON, and verify that it matches the appropriate snapshot from a previous run. This is another early warning system to help catch when someone changes the component but doesn't do anything to update the tests! Let's take a look at the results in our **Test Suite**:

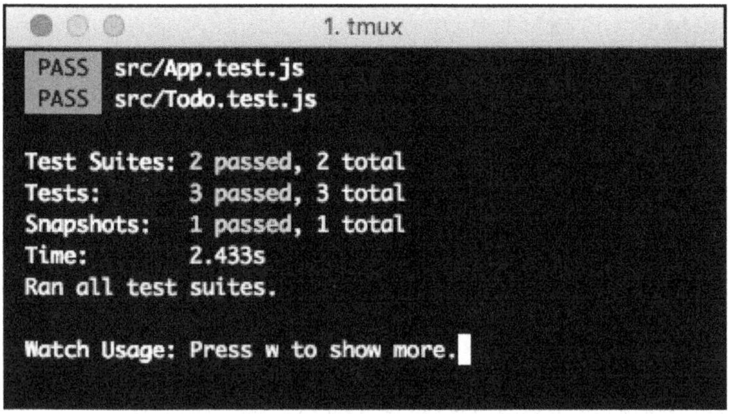

```
1. tmux
 PASS  src/App.test.js
 PASS  src/Todo.test.js

Test Suites: 2 passed, 2 total
Tests:       3 passed, 3 total
Snapshots:   1 passed, 1 total
Time:        2.433s
Ran all test suites.

Watch Usage: Press w to show more.
```

Writing tests for content

We'll also need to make sure that when properties are passed in that modify what's displayed to the user, those properties actually make it into the fully-rendered function! We have a `description` variable that we already set at the top of our describe block. Before we jump too far, we need to write a quick test for our shallow render to make sure that is also working functionally!

What's a shallow render?

A shallow render is basically just a fake render of the component where it only renders the root-level component and nothing else. It's the most minimal rendition of any component that you can use for a test, so we should always use that before we jump into anything else! Let's write our shallow render test first:

```
it("renders a Todo component", () => {
  expect(component.contains(<div className="Todo" />));
});
```

This is a simple test. It just ensures that we render out a `div` with a CSS class of `Todo`, which is the root `div` that gets rendered when we instantiate our `Todo` component in JSX. Otherwise, there are no major surprises here! Following that, we'll need to write some tests that make sure these `props` passed in make it into the `component`:

```
it("contains the description", () => {
  expect(component.text()).toContain(description);
});
```

We already created the shallow rendered version of the `component`, so we're grabbing that component, analyzing the rendered `text` that would get added to the DOM if it were a real render, and then making sure that whatever we put in the description made it in there!

Testing interactions

The last step is to test the actual interactions in your component! We'll need to be able to target each of our buttons, though. If you think back to our `Todo` component's `render()` function, there are two buttons that get created:

```
render() {
  return (
    <div className={this.cssClasses()}>
      {this.state.description}
      <br />
      <button onClick={this.markAsDone}>Mark as Done</button>
      <button onClick={this.removeTodo}>Remove Me</button>
    </div>
  );
}
```

Without any modifications, it would actually be difficult for us to specifically target either of the actual buttons. We'll want a way to target each `button` separately from each other, so let's go into the `Todo` component and add a unique `className` to each button! Add `MarkDone className` to the first `button` and `RemoveTodo className` to the second `button` in the render function in `src/Todo.js`, just like the following code:

```
render() {
  return (
    <div className={this.cssClasses()}>
      {this.props.description}
      <br />
      <button className="MarkDone" onClick={this.markAsDone}>
        Mark as Done
      </button>
      <button className="RemoveTodo" onClick={this.removeTodo}>
```

```
          Remove Me
        </button>
      </div>
    );
  }
```

Save this code and the tests will rerun and it fails? But why? We haven't changed the tests yet! Refer the following screenshot:

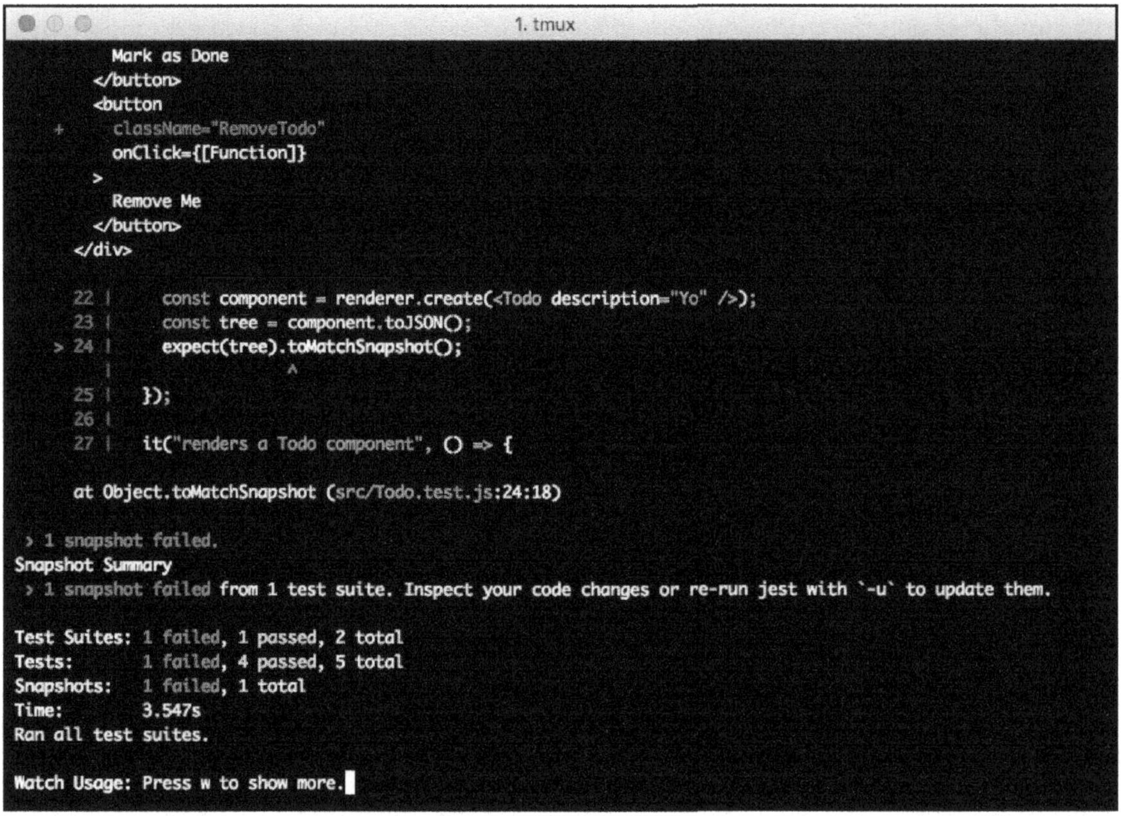

```
1. tmux
        Mark as Done
      </button>
      <button
  +     className="RemoveTodo"
        onClick={[Function]}
      >
        Remove Me
      </button>
    </div>

    22 |     const component = renderer.create(<Todo description="Yo" />);
    23 |     const tree = component.toJSON();
  > 24 |     expect(tree).toMatchSnapshot();
       |                  ^
    25 |   });
    26 |
    27 |   it("renders a Todo component", () => {

    at Object.toMatchSnapshot (src/Todo.test.js:24:18)

 > 1 snapshot failed.
Snapshot Summary
 > 1 snapshot failed from 1 test suite. Inspect your code changes or re-run jest with `-u` to update them.

Test Suites: 1 failed, 1 passed, 2 total
Tests:       1 failed, 4 passed, 5 total
Snapshots:   1 failed, 1 total
Time:        3.547s
Ran all test suites.

Watch Usage: Press w to show more.
```

This is actually doing exactly what it's supposed to! We made some modifications to our component that changed how the component got rendered out. In our case, we're totally okay with these changes, so we'll use another one of our test-watcher commands to update the `snapshot`! Hit *u* and our `snapshot` will get updated and our tests will go back to passing! Finally, we can go back to finishing up our tests for interaction!

Completing our interactivity tests

Now that we can isolate each of the buttons, we can test what happens when each of them is clicked! We'll need to start off by verifying our `MarkDone button` marks that `Todo` as done, which we can do via checking the `state`, as well! Let's take a look at the test and then we'll talk about what it does:

```
it("marks the Todo as done", () => {
  component.find("button.MarkDone").simulate("click");
  expect(component.state("done")).toEqual(true);
});
```

The easiest way to reason about these tests is to say them out loud. If we were to test this behavior as a human, we'd say, find the button that marks the `Todo` as done, click on that button, and then we should expect that `Todo` to be complete! Our code does precisely that! It *finds* the component via a CSS selector that grabs the button that has a CSS class attached to it of `MarkDone` (remember our `render()` function changes earlier). We then simulate a `"click"` event sent to that `button` which targets the `onClick` handler. Finally, we have to use the `state()` function to grab a value out of the component's state, which for us is the `"done"` property in the `state`! If that's now `true`, then we're golden and our tests work!

Returning to our mocked function

We talked a lot about our function mocks but then focused on a bunch of other tests; now it's time for us to revisit our mocked function and actually test it out! Basically, all we need to do is to use a helper function to verify that our mock has been called:

```
it("calls the mock remove function", () => {
  component.find("button.RemoveTodo").simulate("click");
  expect(mockRemoveTodo).toHaveBeenCalled();
});
```

We had our `mockRemoveTodo` function that we had put back up in the top of our describe block:

```
const mockRemoveTodo = jest.fn();
```

We've already seen the `simulate` call in a previous test, so all we do is create the expectation that our mock function has been called, and that's it! With that, we have a very thorough test suite for our `Todo` component, and everything we do from here are just slightly more complicated variations of the same tests! Seven total **Tests**, two **Test Suites**, and one **Snapshots** test—all working perfectly! Refer the following screenshot:

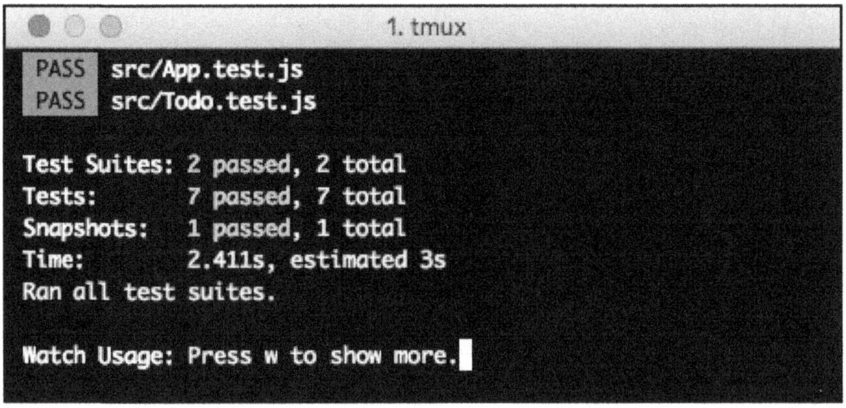

```
1. tmux
PASS  src/App.test.js
PASS  src/Todo.test.js

Test Suites: 2 passed, 2 total
Tests:       7 passed, 7 total
Snapshots:   1 passed, 1 total
Time:        2.411s, estimated 3s
Ran all test suites.

Watch Usage: Press w to show more.
```

Before we move on, let's verify the full test suite for `src/Todo.test.js`:

```
import React from "react";
import ReactDOM from "react-dom";
import { shallow } from "enzyme";
import renderer from "react-test-renderer";

import Todo from "./Todo";

describe(Todo, () => {
  const description = "New Todo";
  const mockRemoveTodo = jest.fn();
  const component = shallow(
    <Todo description={description} removeTodo={mockRemoveTodo} />
  );

  it("renders without crashing", () => {
    const div = document.createElement("div");
    ReactDOM.render(<Todo />, div);
    ReactDOM.unmountComponentAtNode(div);
  });

  it("renders and matches our snapshot", () => {
    const component = renderer.create(<Todo description="Yo" />);
    const tree = component.toJSON();
    expect(tree).toMatchSnapshot();
```

```
  });

  it("renders a Todo component", () => {
    expect(component.contains(<div className="Todo" />));
  });

  it("contains the description", () => {
    expect(component.text()).toContain(description);
  });

  it("marks the Todo as done", () => {
    component.find("button.MarkDone").simulate("click");
    expect(component.state("done")).toEqual(true);
  });

  it("calls the mock remove function", () => {
    component.find("button.RemoveTodo").simulate("click");
    expect(mockRemoveTodo).toHaveBeenCalled();
  });
});
```

Let's now add some tests for `TodoList` as well!

Adding tests for TodoList

We'll start off by adding a framework to put the rest of our `TodoList` tests on! We'll need our standard imports and tests for rendering, snapshots, and shallow components! We'll start off with this scaffold for `src/TodoList.test.js`:

```
import React from "react";
import ReactDOM from "react-dom";
import { shallow } from "enzyme";
import renderer from "react-test-renderer";

import TodoList from "./TodoList";
import NewTodo from "./NewTodo";
import Todo from "./Todo";

describe(TodoList, () => {
  const component = shallow(<TodoList />);

  it("renders without crashing", () => {
    const div = document.createElement("div");
    ReactDOM.render(<TodoList />, div);
    ReactDOM.unmountComponentAtNode(div);
  });
```

```
  it("renders and matches our snapshot", () => {
    const component = renderer.create(<TodoList />);
    const tree = component.toJSON();
    expect(tree).toMatchSnapshot();
  });

  it("renders a TodoList component", () => {
    expect(component.contains(<div className="TodoList" />));
  });
});
```

We covered these tests previously, so there's not much we'll need to jump into, but we will want to make sure that, since our `render()` call includes a `NewTodo` component and we've imported that `component` at the top of our file, we have a test that verifies there's a single `NewTodo` in the tree:

```
  it("includes a NewTodo component", () => {
    expect(component.find(NewTodo)).toHaveLength(1);
  });
```

We'll also need to verify how many `Todo` components appear in our `TodoList`, but there's a little bit of a more complicated problem we have to solve with this test. If you remember, the state's `"items"` property in `TodoList` determines what `Todo`s should appear, so we'll check the state versus the component's `find` function to see that the two are in sync with each other:

```
  it("renders the correct number of Todo components", () => {
    const todoCount = component.state("items").length;
    expect(component.find(Todo)).toHaveLength(todoCount);
  });
```

Our `component` already gets rendered out via the `shallow()` call, so we'll use the `state()` call to verify the length of the items and find the equal number of `Todo` components. We'll also need to test our `addTodo` function of `TodoList`:

```
  it("adds another Todo when the addTodo function is called", () => {
    const before = component.find(Todo).length;
    component.instance().addTodo("A new item");
    const after = component.find(Todo).length;
    expect(after).toBeGreaterThan(before);
  });
```

There's some new functionality in here that might be slightly complicated, so let's talk a little bit about it! We start off by finding out how many Todos already exist, since after we add another item we should expect that to be what we started with, plus another one! After that, we'll want to call `addTodo()` on the component, but to do that we need to jump down into the actual living context of `component`. We can do that via the `instance()` call, which allows us to call any function on the `component` without having to simulate any button clicks! After we call `addTodo`, we grab the list of all of the Todos that exist on the function and expect it to be more than what we originally started with! This is a really important and great way to write our tests; we never hardcode the number of Todos or anything else; instead, we check relative values after events happen! This eliminates weird scenarios where someone changes the default or initial state for our components and breaks our tests as a direct result!

Finally, we need to implement a `removeTodo` test, which is just the reverse operation from the test we previously wrote:

```
  it("removes a Todo from the list when the remove todo function is
called", () => {
    const before = component.find(Todo).length;
    const removeMe = component.state("items")[0];
    component.instance().removeTodo(removeMe);
    const after = component.find(Todo).length;
    expect(after).toBeLessThan(before);
  });
```

The only notable difference is the fact that `removeTodo` needs an actual item to remove, so we have to grab one of the items out of the list and remove that specifically by passing that value into the `removeTodo` function!

After all is said and done, we should have a full test suite for `TodoList.test.js` that looks like this:

```
import React from "react";
import ReactDOM from "react-dom";
import { shallow } from "enzyme";
import renderer from "react-test-renderer";

import TodoList from "./TodoList";
import NewTodo from "./NewTodo";
import Todo from "./Todo";

describe(TodoList, () => {
  const component = shallow(<TodoList />);

  it("renders without crashing", () => {
```

```
    const div = document.createElement("div");
    ReactDOM.render(<TodoList />, div);
    ReactDOM.unmountComponentAtNode(div);
  });

  it("renders and matches our snapshot", () => {
    const component = renderer.create(<TodoList />);
    const tree = component.toJSON();
    expect(tree).toMatchSnapshot();
  });

  it("renders a TodoList component", () => {
    expect(component.contains(<div className="TodoList" />));
  });

  it("includes a NewTodo component", () => {
    expect(component.find(NewTodo)).toHaveLength(1);
  });

  it("renders the correct number of Todo components", () => {
    const todoCount = component.state("items").length;
    expect(component.find(Todo)).toHaveLength(todoCount);
  });

  it("adds another Todo when the addTodo function is called", () => {
    const before = component.find(Todo).length;
    component.instance().addTodo("A new item");
    const after = component.find(Todo).length;
    expect(after).toBeGreaterThan(before);
  });

  it("removes a Todo from the list when the remove todo function is
called", () => {
    const before = component.find(Todo).length;
    const removeMe = component.state("items")[0];
    component.instance().removeTodo(removeMe);
    const after = component.find(Todo).length;
    expect(after).toBeLessThan(before);
  });
});
```

Adding tests for NewTodo

At last, we can add our final test suite and make sure `NewTodo` is covered as well. For the most part, we'll work with the same skeleton we already have and have used before. Create `src/NewTodo.test.js` and give it the following skeleton:

```
import React from "react";
import ReactDOM from "react-dom";
import { shallow } from "enzyme";
import renderer from "react-test-renderer";

import NewTodo from "./NewTodo";

describe(NewTodo, () => {
  const mockAddTodo = jest.fn();
  const component = shallow(<NewTodo addTodo={mockAddTodo} />);

  it("renders without crashing", () => {
    const div = document.createElement("div");
    ReactDOM.render(<NewTodo addTodo={mockAddTodo} />, div);
    ReactDOM.unmountComponentAtNode(div);
  });

  it("renders and matches our snapshot", () => {
    const component = renderer.create(<NewTodo addTodo={mockAddTodo} />);
    const tree = component.toJSON();
    expect(tree).toMatchSnapshot();
  });

  it("renders a Todo component", () => {
    expect(component.contains(<div className="NewTodo" />));
  });
});
```

We'll also want to modify the tests we wrote that check our content, since we should at least make sure that the there's still a text field and a `button` as part of the form:

```
it('contains the form', () => {
  expect(component.find('input')).toHaveLength(1);
  expect(component.find('button')).toHaveLength(1);
});
```

We'll also want to test our mocked addTodo function:

```
it("calls the passed in addTodo function when add button is clicked", ()
=> {
  component.find("button").simulate("click");
  expect(mockAddTodo).toBeCalled();
});
```

This is essentially identical to what we did in the Todo component suite. We'll need a test for our handleUpdate function, which should modify the "item" state property to the faked input value:

```
it("updates the form when keys are pressed", () => {
  const updateKey = "New Todo";
  component.instance().handleUpdate({ target: { value: updateKey } });
  expect(component.state("item")).toEqual(updateKey);
});
```

The structure of the handleUpdate argument is a little wacky, so we need to make sure we're passing in an object that's compatible with the handleUpdate function that we wrote, which is as follows:

```
handleUpdate(event) {
  this.setState({ item: event.target.value });
}
```

We then use the state function to verify that "item" now matches what we passed in! We'll close out our test-writing escapade by verifying that when the button to add an item is clicked that the value in the "item" state key is reset to blank:

```
it("blanks out the Todo Name when the button is clicked", () => {
const updateKey = "I should be empty";
component.instance().handleUpdate({ target: { value: updateKey } });
expect(component.state("item")).toEqual(updateKey);
component.find("button").simulate("click");
expect(component.state("item")).toHaveLength(0);
});
```

We need to verify that we're being thorough with our test by making sure the component has a value first and then is reset to blank. If we don't, we wouldn't have any way to verify that our test was working the way we're expecting!

The full test suite is provided here:

```
import React from "react";
import ReactDOM from "react-dom";
import { shallow } from "enzyme";
import renderer from "react-test-renderer";

import NewTodo from "./NewTodo";

describe(NewTodo, () => {
 const mockAddTodo = jest.fn();
 const component = shallow(<NewTodo addTodo={mockAddTodo} />);

 it("renders without crashing", () => {
 const div = document.createElement("div");
 ReactDOM.render(<NewTodo addTodo={mockAddTodo} />, div);
 ReactDOM.unmountComponentAtNode(div);
 });

 it("renders and matches our snapshot", () => {
 const component = renderer.create(<NewTodo addTodo={mockAddTodo} />);
 const tree = component.toJSON();
 expect(tree).toMatchSnapshot();
 });

 it("renders a Todo component", () => {
 expect(component.contains(<div className="NewTodo" />));
 });

 it("contains the form", () => {
 expect(component.find("input")).toHaveLength(1);
 expect(component.find("button")).toHaveLength(1);
 });

 it("calls the passed in addTodo function when add button is clicked", ()
=> {
 component.find("button").simulate("click");
 expect(mockAddTodo).toBeCalled();
 });

 it("updates the form when keys are pressed", () => {
 const updateKey = "New Todo";
 component.instance().handleUpdate({ target: { value: updateKey } });
 expect(component.state("item")).toEqual(updateKey);
 });

 it("blanks out the Todo Name when the button is clicked", () => {
 const updateKey = "I should be empty";
```

```
    component.instance().handleUpdate({ target: { value: updateKey } });
    expect(component.state("item")).toEqual(updateKey);
    component.find("button").simulate("click");
    expect(component.state("item")).toHaveLength(0);
  });
});
```

The final result of all of our tests, if you've been following along, should be the following **Test Suite** results:

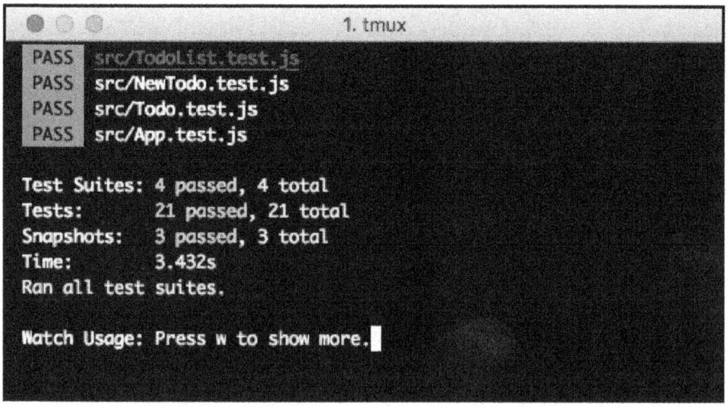

```
1. tmux
PASS  src/TodoList.test.js
PASS  src/NewTodo.test.js
PASS  src/Todo.test.js
PASS  src/App.test.js

Test Suites: 4 passed, 4 total
Tests:       21 passed, 21 total
Snapshots:   3 passed, 3 total
Time:        3.432s
Ran all test suites.

Watch Usage: Press w to show more.
```

Summary

Testing is something that's absolutely critical to the overall health of your application! It ensures your development cycles are sane and your deploys are not incredibly dangerous. Your behavior can be tested, verified, and you can be confident in what your application is doing at any point in time without ever needing to open up a browser!

This is something that used to be a nightmare to do. The React test setup was a function that people generally hated given how much of a time commitment it took and how finicky it ended up being after the setup was done. One misstep or bad configuration change and the entire test harness framework could fall apart completely!

Be prepared to write a lot of tests if you write a production-ready React application! It's a great software engineering practice to be do whenever you're doing anything code-wise, and React is no different!

In the next chapter, we'll dive into cleaning up the visual design of our project with the new CSS module and the SASS support that's built into Create React App's latest version, and we'll incorporate a major CSS framework as well!

5
Applying Modern CSS to Create React App Projects

As we've been working on our project, we've been focusing very heavily on the functionality, but overall we have been perhaps slightly less focused on how everything actually looks! While this is fine for establishing functionality and making everything flow nicely at the start of the project, any designers working on the project will be ready to scream at this point!

Let's appease our design team, whether it's an actual team or just ourselves, by spending a little bit of time cleaning up the visual appeal of our project! In relation to our current design, while it's not necessarily hideous, it certainly leaves a lot to be desired!

So, how do we improve our application's design in a safe and sound way? Well, previously with Create React App, you actually didn't have a lot of options to be able to clean things up visually. You were frequently at the whims and mercy of random **Cascading Style Sheets** (**CSS**) project maintainers, and trying to get other libraries, frameworks, or preprocessors involved in the project compilation process was frequently a nightmare.

A **preprocessor** in the context of Create React App is basically one of the steps in the build process. In this case, we're talking about something that takes some of the style code (CSS or another format), compiles it down to basic CSS, and adds it to the output of the build process.

Over the span of this chapter, we'll be covering materials that span the gamut of style-related functionality and highlighting what is, in my mind, one of the best new features in Create React App: support for CSS Modules and SASS. Specifically, we'll be covering the following topics:

- The different ways to get CSS into our project
- A brief history of CSS in Create React App projects
- Introducing CSS Modules

- Introducing SASS to our project
- Mixing CSS Modules and SASS together
- Integrating CSS Modules and SASS into our project
- Integrating CSS frameworks into our project
- Cleaning up our tests after modifying the design

What tools are available?

Create React App, by default, supports us getting CSS into our application in a number of different ways.

We can get CSS directly into our components by writing a `style` attribute and giving it some arbitrary CSS, as in the following code:

```
const Example = () => {
  return (
    <div className="Example" style="border: 1px solid red;">
      Hello
    </div>
  );
};
```

This will give us a little `div` with the word `Hello` in it, surrounded by a single-pixel red line for the border. While this is something you technically can do, generally speaking, you should avoid it. Using inline style statements like the preceding example makes it hard to keep your styles organized and track them down when formatting does go awry. Plus, if a designer or another non-developer needs to update the look and feel (for example, if the standard colors for things change), they will have to search to find where this one random little one-pixel red border is coming from!

We can also create `.css` files and then `import` them into our project via a statement like the following:

```
import "./someStyle.css";
```

This is a technique that you've seen used before and that we've used a great deal in our application. It's useful, of course, and allows us some small amount of separation of code and styles, but it doesn't give us everything that we need. In fact, it actually introduces a new problem that we now have to solve, and one that can make fixing your projects and cleaning up the visual display of your projects incredibly frustrating and difficult over time: CSS conflicts!

CSS conflicts can ruin your application

What is a CSS conflict? Basically, when you import a CSS file into one of your components, it doesn't really limit it to one specific file; it gets added to the global CSS definitions instead. This means that if you define a particular style in one place, it might override or conflict with a totally different style in a different place. These style sheets get imported in some particular order, depending on how the code is loaded into your application overall, and everything ends up getting added to one big giant style sheet by the time your browser loads it all in.

As you can imagine, if everything is getting added to one gigantic file and there's no real differentiation between different files and how everything gets loaded, you will likely run into issues periodically where something that has been carelessly named ends up breaking everything!

A quick example of CSS conflicts

The easiest way to understand this is to see it in action. For the most part, we were pretty smart and safe about how we named our CSS files, but we did run into one giant gotcha: our `Divider` component defines a global style for all `hr` tags, regardless of where they appear. Let's head back into `src/Todo.js`, and change our `render` function to place an `hr` tag in between the `description` and the `button`:

```
render() {
  return (
    <div className={this.cssClasses()}>
      {this.state.description}
      <br />
      <hr />
      <button className="MarkDone" onClick={this.markAsDone}>
        Mark as Done
      </button>
      <button className="RemoveTodo" onClick={this.removeTodo}>
        Remove Me
      </button>
    </div>
  );
}
```

Note that we have not added any style at all to this yet! Save the file and reload it, and despite us having never defined a style for `hr` tags in the `Todo` component, we'll see that it has inherited the style of the `Divider` components! Refer to the following screenshot:

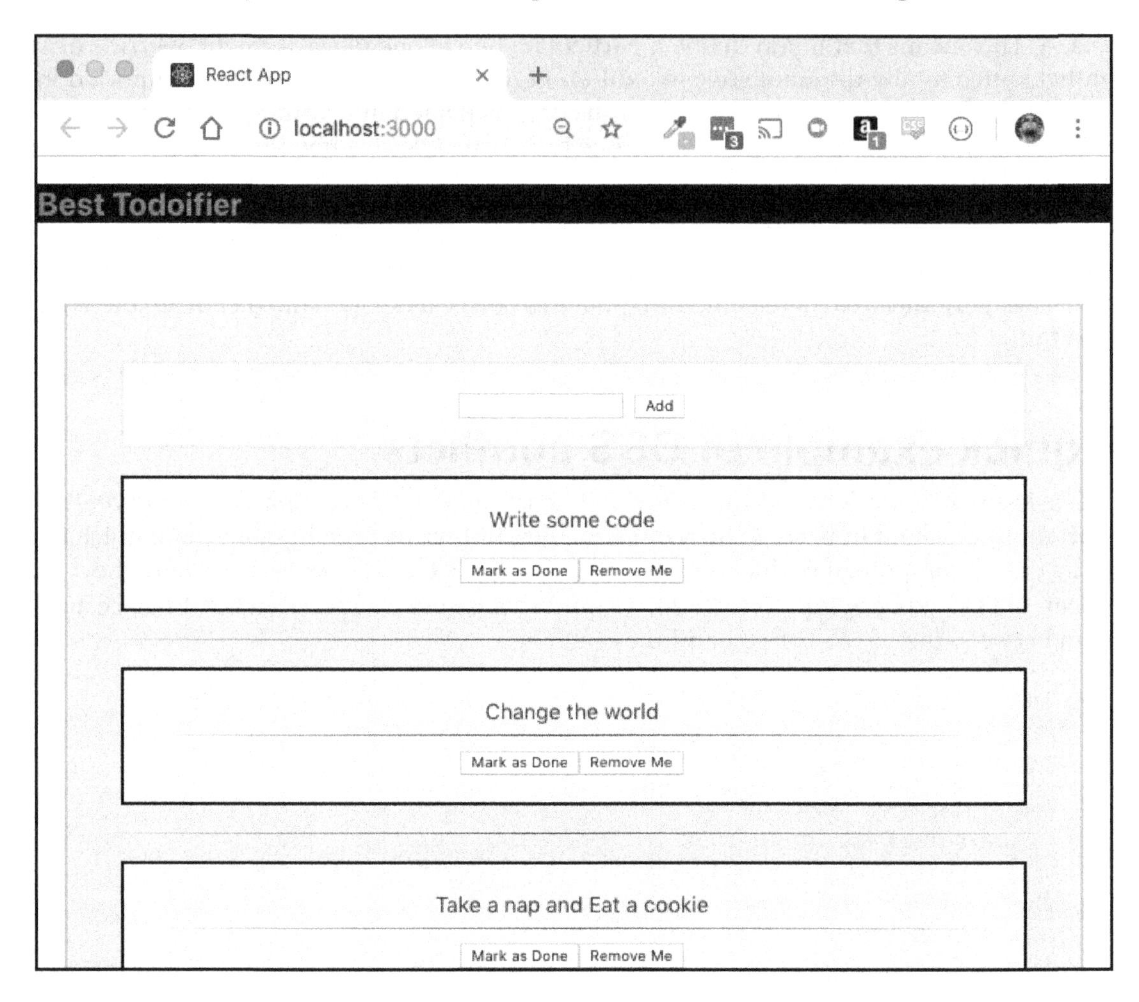

But that's not what we wanted! While that's a pretty nice divider, maybe we want ours to have a different color! For the sake of comparison, we'll say that we want the dividers inside of the `Todo` component to be solid red lines but we want the other ones to stay the same. We'll add the following CSS to `src/Todo.css` to change our `hr` tag to red instead by changing the `border` color:

```
hr {
  border: 2px solid red;
}
```

Save and reload, and nothing happens? That's odd. The code is correct and it's definitely importing the CSS into our application correctly. Just as a sanity check, we'll change the `hr` tag to a `div` tag to make sure it adds a red border to our `Todo div` tags:

```
div {
  border: 2px solid red;
}
```

Save and reload, and you should now see this:

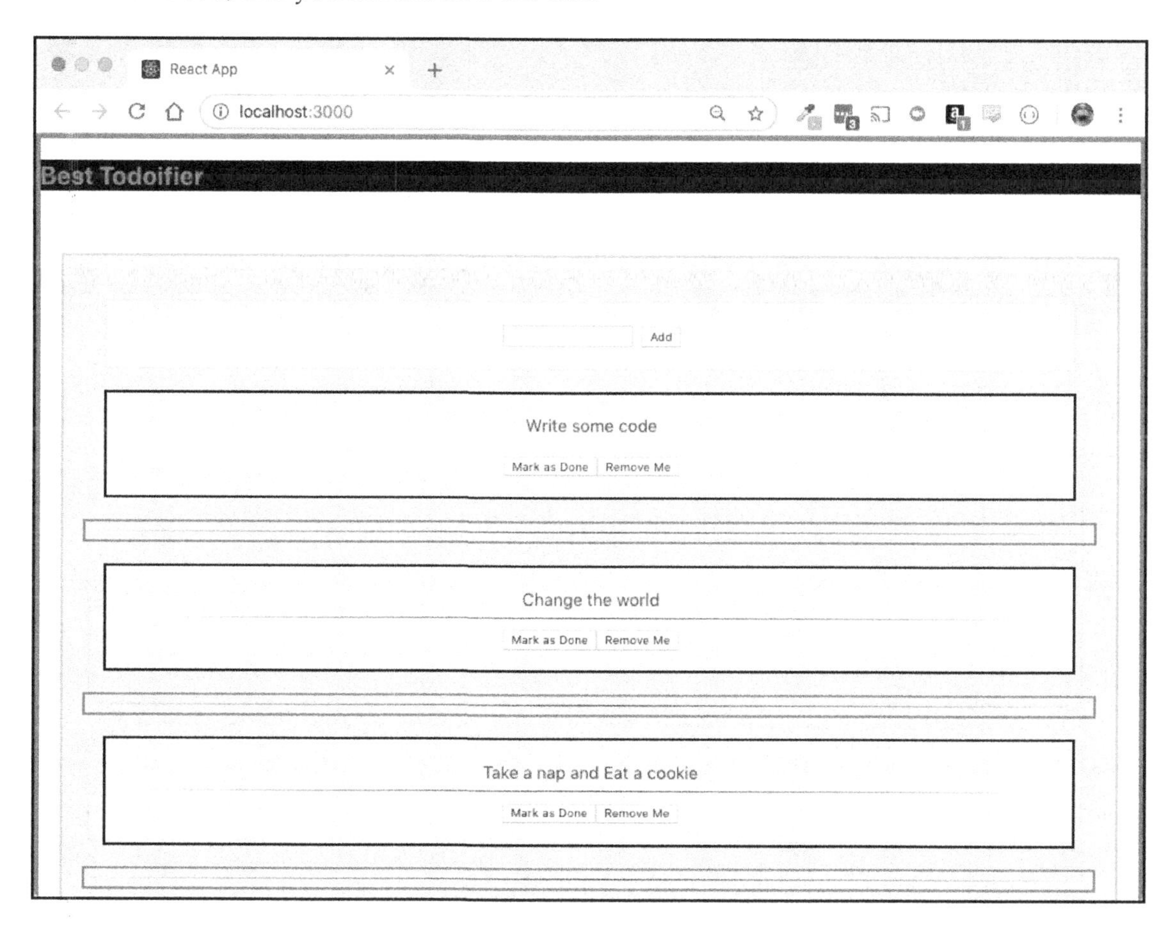

Yikes, that's not what we wanted! It's added borders to *every* `div` on the page instead of just the `div` tag in our `Todo` component! Well, at least we've figured out there's nothing weird with the code, it's just something with how the CSS is getting loaded. It's easy to fix; we'll just toss an `!important` flag on the end of our `src/Todo.css` file's `hr` definition and call it a day!

The `!important` flag is a way to force CSS to prioritize this directive over other directives. It's also a great way to make your application a living nightmare to maintain over time; avoid using this whenever you possibly can!

Back in `src/Todo.css`, we'll commit our CSS crime by tossing an `!important` flag at the end of the `hr` block:

```
hr {
  border: 2px solid red !important;
}
```

There we go! Save and reload, and we will see the following output:

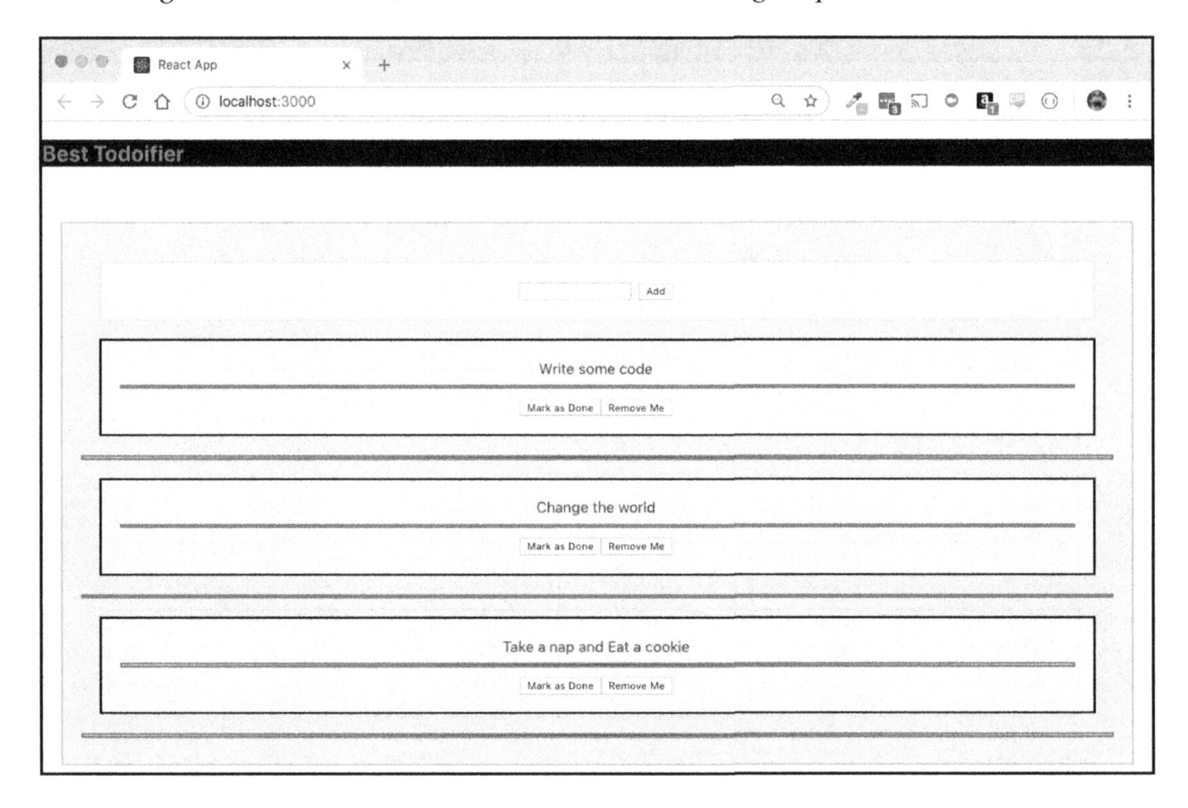

Now, we've ruined everything. Yikes! Hopefully our design team won't just completely disown us for this, right? They're really good at CSS, so they'll fix things! Well, they'll fix things after they're done yelling at us for botching the site's design inside of the code in a way that is incredibly difficult for a non-developer to track down.

The good news is that there is a different way to handle this situation in a way that works very well and prevents exactly this sort of scenario in the future! It is something that has been an absolute godsend to those of us that have been working on shared frontend development projects, which might have multiple different CSS files to have to search through to find the single CSS file that's causing a major design headache!

Introducing CSS Modules

The first of these are CSS Modules, and in Create React App 2 and higher, you don't need to do anything at all to start taking advantage of it immediately. CSS Modules give you the ability to modularize any CSS code that you import in a way that prevents introducing global, overlapping namespaces, despite the fact that the end result is still just one giant CSS file.

That being said, it's also not just going to immediately work in your project if you don't turn anything on or organize your code a little bit better. Right now, we've been placing all of our code directly into the `src/` directory, resulting in a scenario where the `root` folder is going to keep growing and growing over time until it gets so large and unwieldy that you'll never be able to find anything.

Better project organization

Let's start off by cleaning up our directory structure in our project a little bit better. There are a million different ways to do this and, honestly, they all have their own merits and flaws. We're going to adopt a very simple structure right now since this project is not really going to be terribly large, so keeping things simple and building up is very easy to do with this structure. What we're going to do is just separate out each component that has CSS and JavaScript code into their own folders. We'll start off by creating `NewTodo`, `Todo`, `App`, `TodoList`, and `Divider` folders and placing all of their related code in each of those. We'll also need to create a new file in each of these directories called `index.js`, which will be responsible for only importing and exporting the appropriate component. For example, the `App` index file (`src/App/index.js`) will look like this:

```
import App from "./App";
export default App;
```

The new index file of `Todo` (`src/Todo/index.js`) will look like this:

```
import Todo from "./Todo";
export default Todo;
```

You can probably guess what the index files `NewTodo`, `TodoList`, and `Divider` will look like as well, based on this pattern!

Next, we'll need to change each place that these files are referenced to make it easier to import all of them. This will unfortunately be a little bit of grunt work, but we'll need to do it all the same to make sure we don't break anything in the process.

First, in `src/App/App.js`, change the `TodoList import` component to the following:

```
import TodoList from "../TodoList";
```

There's nothing we need to do for `Divider` since it is a component with no imports. `NewTodo` and `Todo` are of a similar type, so we can skip them as well. `src/TodoList/TodoList.js`, on the other hand, has a lot we need to deal with, since it's one of our highest-level components and imports a lot:

```
import Todo from "../Todo";
import NewTodo from "../NewTodo";
import Divider from "../Divider";
```

But that's not all. Our test file, `src/TodoList/TodoList.test.js`, also needs to be modified to include these new paths for our files or else our tests will fail! We'll need nearly the same list of imports as earlier:

```
import TodoList from "./TodoList";
import NewTodo from "../NewTodo";
import Todo from "../Todo";
```

Now, when you reload your application, your code should still be working just fine, your tests should all pass, and everything should be cleanly separated out! This makes our lives easier for a number of reasons, but when we're talking about working with other developers or designers, this makes things a godsend for them since they can figure out exactly what CSS to modify when they need to fix things up! Our full project structure should now look like this:

```
src/
  App/
    App.css
    App.js
    App.test.js
    index.js
  Divider/
    Divider.css
    Divider.js
    index.js
  NewTodo/
```

```
    NewTodo.css
    NewTodo.js
    NewTodo.test.js
    index.js
  Todo/
    Todo.css
    Todo.js
    Todo.test.js
    index.js
  TodoList/
    TodoList.css
    TodoList.js
    TodoList.test.js
    index.js
  index.css
  index.js
  setupTests.js
  ... etc ...
```

How to use CSS Modules

It's time for us to jump right into incorporating CSS Modules into our project. Right now, we haven't set up anything to start using CSS Modules, so we'll need to make a few changes to make this work. Think back to our `Todo` CSS conflict, where introducing some conflicting CSS namespaces and poor choices around the use of the `!important` flag introduced a nightmare situation.

Instead, let's start taking advantage of CSS Modules! We can actually mix the old way of doing things and the new way as well, but it'd be nice to take things a step further and use CSS Modules all the way.

Introducing CSS Modules to our application

If we want to use CSS Modules, there are a few simple guidelines that we need to follow. The first is that we need to name our files `[whatever].module.css`, instead of `[whatever].css`. The next thing we need to do is to make sure that our styles are named simply and are easy to reference. Let's start off by following these conventions and by renaming our CSS file for `Todo` as `src/Todo/Todo.module.css`, and then we'll change the contents a tiny bit:

```
.todo {
  border: 2px solid black;
  text-align: center;
```

```
  background: #f5f5f5;
  color: #333;
  margin: 20px;
  padding: 20px;
}

.done {
  background: #f5a5a5;
}
```

CSS Module guidelines prefer that you use **camelCase** for naming conventions, so `Done` and `Todo` will become `done` and `todo`, respectively. Something like `NewTodo` will instead become `newTodo` as well!

Next, we'll open up `src/Todo/Todo.js` to take advantage of CSS Modules instead. We created a helper function in our `Todo` component called `cssClasses()`, which returns the styles we should be using in our component, and there's not much we need to change to make this all work exactly the same as earlier. We'll need to change our `import` statement at the top as well, since we renamed the file and are changing how our CSS is getting loaded into our code! Take a look at the following:

```
import styles from "./Todo.module.css";
```

This enables our code to take advantage of any class names defined in `Todo.module.css` by referencing them as `styles.[className]`. For example, in the previous file, we defined two CSS class names: `todo` and `done`, so we can now reference them in our component via `styles.Todo` and `styles.done`. We'll need to change the `cssClasses()` function to use this, so let's make those exact changes now. In `src/Todo/Todo.js`, our `cssClasses()` function should now read as follows:

```
  cssClasses() {
    let classes = [styles.todo];
    if (this.state.done) {
      classes = [...classes, styles.done];
    }
    return classes.join(' ');
  }
```

Save and reload, and our application should be back to normal! There's more we can do here, though, so let's return back to our conflict scenario. If you remember, the problem was that we needed to be able to change the `hr` tags inside of the `todo` components to have their own styles and effects, but not affect everything else and also not have to use the `!important` flag if we can avoid it. Head back into `src/Todo/Todo.module.css` and add the following block for our `hr` tag, which we'll give a new class of `redDivider`:

```
.redDivider {
  border: 2px solid red;
}
```

And finally, return back to our `render()` function in `src/Todo/Todo.js`, and change our `render()` function's `hr` tag inclusion to the following:

```
<hr className={styles.redDivider} />
```

Save and reload, and now we should have fully compartmentalized CSS code without worrying about collisions and global namespaces! Refer to the following screenshot:

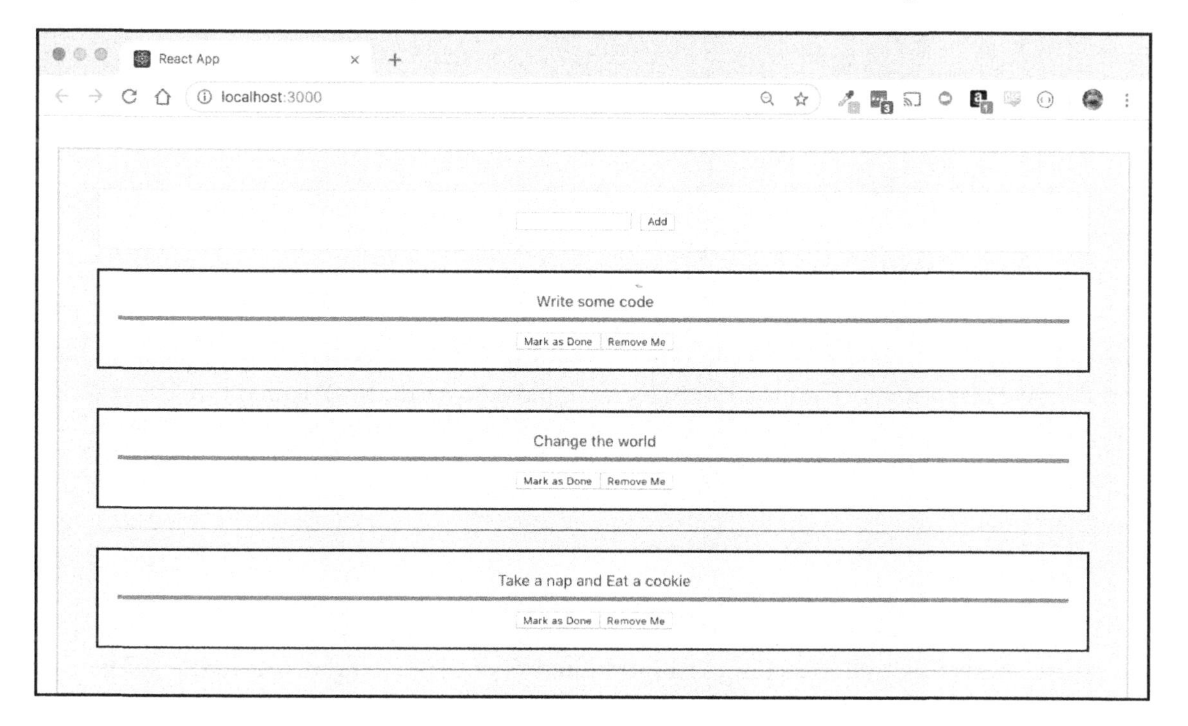

Composability with CSS Modules

That's not all that CSS Modules give us, although it's certainly one of the great parts of CSS Modules that we get immediately and with no fuss (seriously, we wrote zero configuration to make all of it happen; it was all just code). We also get CSS composability, which is the ability to inherit CSS classes off of other classes, whether they're in the main file or not! This can be incredibly useful when you're setting up more complicated nested components that all need to handle slightly different style sheets, but are not wildly different from each other. Let's say we want to have the ability to mark some components as `critical` instead of just regular Todos.

We don't want to change too much about the component; we want it to inherit the same basic rules as all of the other Todos. We'll need to set up some code to make this happen. Back in `src/Todo/Todo.js`, we're going to make some modifications to allow a new state property of `critical`. We'll start off in the `constructor` component, where we'll add our new `state` property and a `bind` tag for a function:

```
constructor(props) {
  super(props);
  this.state = {
    done: false,
    critical: false
  };

  this.markAsDone = this.markAsDone.bind(this);
  this.removeTodo = this.removeTodo.bind(this);
  this.markCritical = this.markCritical.bind(this);
}
```

We add a new `critical` property in our `state` property, set it to a default value of `false`, and then we also reference a function (which we haven't written yet) called `markCritical`, and we bind `this`, since we'll be using it in an event handler later. Next, we'll tackle the `markCritical()` function:

```
markCritical() {
  this.setState({ critical: true });
}
```

We'll also need to modify our `cssClasses()` function so that it can react to this new `state` property. To demonstrate the composability function of CSS Modules, we'll set it so that `classes` is originally an empty array, and then the first item either becomes `critical` or `todo`, depending on whether or not the item is marked as `critical`:

```
cssClasses() {
  let classes = [];
```

```
    if (this.state.critical) {
      classes = [styles.critical];
    } else {
      classes = [styles.todo];
    }
    if (this.state.done) {
      classes = [...classes, styles.done];
    }
    return classes.join(' ');
  }
```

And finally, in our `render` function, we'll create the `button` tag to mark items as `critical`:

```
  render() {
    return (
      <div className={this.cssClasses()}>
        {this.props.description}
        <br />
        <hr className={styles.hr} />
        <button className="MarkDone" onClick={this.markAsDone}>
          Mark as Done
        </button>
        <button className="RemoveTodo" onClick={this.removeTodo}>
          Remove Me
        </button>
        <button className="MarkCritical" onClick={this.markCritical}>
          Mark as Critical
        </button>
      </div>
    );
  }
```

We're not quite done yet, although we're at least 90% of the way there. We'll also want to go back to `src/Todo/Todo.module.css` and add a new block for the `critical` class name, and we'll use our composable property as well:

```
.critical {
  composes: todo;
  border: 4px dashed red;
}
```

To use composition, all you need to do is add a new CSS property called `composes` and give it a class name (or multiple class names) that you want it to compose. Compose, in this case, is a fancy way of saying that it inherits the behavior of the other class names and allows you to override others. In the previous case, we're saying `critical` is a CSS module class that is composed of a `todo` model as the base, and adds a `border` component of a big red dashed line since, well, we'll just say that this means it is `critical`. This previous code is the equivalent of us writing out the following:

```
.critical {
  text-align: center;
  background: #f5f5f5;
  color: #333;
  margin: 20px;
  padding: 20px;
  border: 4px dashed red;
}
```

Save and reload, as always, and you should be able to mark items as **Mark as Done**, **Mark as Critical**, or both, or remove them by clicking **Remove Me**, as in the following screenshot:

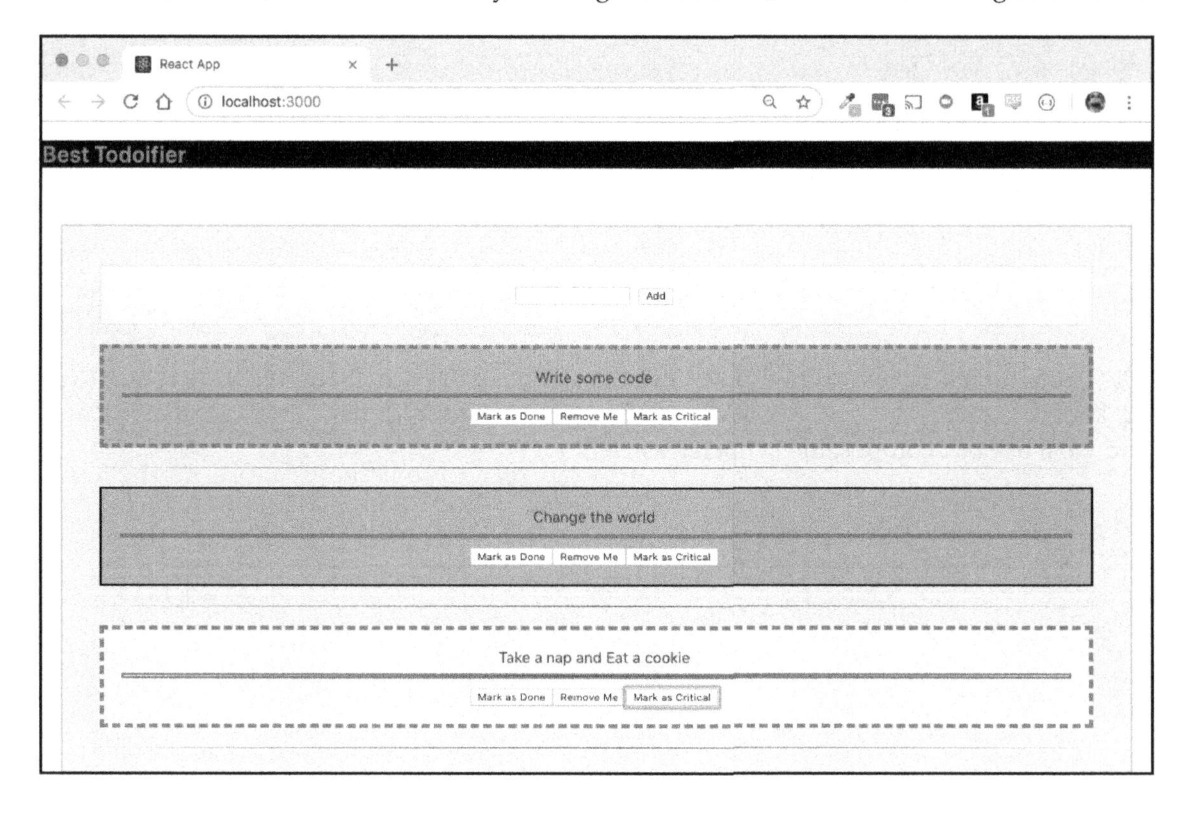

And that about covers it for our brief introduction to CSS Modules! There's certainly more that you could cover over time, but this is more intended to be a quickstart guide and we could probably fill up a second book just on CSS techniques and libraries!

Before you move on, you'll also want to quickly update your snapshots for your tests by hitting *U* in the `yarn test` screen!

Introducing SASS to our project

That's not all that the Create React App added support for as part of Create React App 2! By very popular demand, the Create React App team added in support for SASS pre-processing as well! Often, you'd pretty much be guaranteed that you'd need to eject your project as soon as you wanted to start working with any SASS in your project.

What is SASS?

Let's talk a little bit about what SASS actually is, since it's a pretty important thing to cover. Otherwise, you'd have no connection to why this is worth the effort (even though, to be fair, it is very little effort to integrate into your Create React App projects). SASS is essentially CSS with extended feature support. When I say *extended feature support* here, though, I mean it! SASS supports the following feature set, which is missing in CSS, and which includes the following:

- Variables
- Nesting
- Partial CSS files
- Import support
- Mixins
- Extensions and inheritance
- Operators and calculations

This feature set alone makes including SASS worth it on nearly any complicated frontend project that you might be working with, and honestly after using SASS for a long time and then not having it, it's hard to ever want to go back to vanilla CSS. So, let's start getting some SASS into our project!

Installing and configuring SASS

The good news is that getting SASS support working in a Create React App project is incredibly simple! We first need to install it via `yarn`, or `npm` first. We've used `yarn` for everything else so we'll stick to it:

```
$ yarn add node-sass
```

We'll see a *ton* of output from it, but assuming there are no errors and everything goes well, we should be able to restart our development server and get started with some SASS. Let's create a more general utility SASS file that will be responsible for storing standardized colors that we'll want to use throughout our application, and something to store that neat gradient `hr` pattern in case we want to use it elsewhere.

We'll also change some of the colors that we're using so that there is some red, green, and blue, depending on whether the item is critical, done, or neither, respectively. In addition, we'll need to change up our project a little bit and add a new file to have a concept of some shared styles and colors. So, let's begin:

1. Create a new file, `src/shared.scss`, in our project and give it the following body:

```
$todo-critical: #f5a5a5;
$todo-normal: #a5a5f5;
$todo-complete: #a5f5a5;
$fancy-gradient: linear-gradient(
  to right,
  rgba(0, 0, 0, 0),
  rgba(0, 0, 0, 0.8),
  rgba(0, 0, 0, 0)
);
```

2. Next, hop over to `src/Divider/Divider.css` and rename the file to `src/Divider/Divider.scss`. Next, we'll change the reference to `Divider.css` in `src/Divider/Divider.js`, as follows:

```
import "./Divider.scss";
```

3. Now we'll need to change up the code in `Divider.scss` to import in our shared variables file and use a variable as part of it:

   ```
   @import "../shared";

   hr {
     border: 0;
     height: 1px;
     background-image: $fancy-gradient;
   }
   ```

   So, we import in our new shared SASS file in `src/`, and then the `background-image` value just references the `$fancy-gradient` variable that we created, which means we can now recreate that fancy gradient whenever we need to without having to rewrite it over and over!

4. Save and reload, and you should see that nothing major has changed!

This is a pretty good example of introducing SASS where it just replaces our standard CSS, but what about when we start to introduce CSS Modules?

Mixing SASS and CSS Modules

The good news is that it's basically no more complicated to introduce SASS to CSS Modules in Create React App. In fact, the steps are borderline identical! So, if we want to start mixing the two, all we need to do is rename some files and change how our imports are handled. Let's see this in action:

1. First, head back to our `src/Todo/Todo.module.css` file and make a very minor modification. Specifically, let's rename it `src/Todo/Todo.module.scss`. Next, we need to change our `import` statement in `src/Todo/Todo.js`, otherwise the whole thing will fall apart:

   ```
   import styles from "./Todo.module.scss";
   ```

2. Now, we should have our SASS working for CSS Modules with the `Todo` component, so let's start taking advantage of it. Again, we'll need to `import` our `shared` file into this SASS file as well. Note the following back in `src/Todo/Todo.module.scss`:

   ```
   @import '../shared';
   ```

3. Next, we'll need to start changing the references to our various background colors. We'll change the background for regular Todos to `$todo-normal`. Then, we'll change the finished `Todo` background to `$todo-complete`. Finally, we'll want to change the `critical` items to `$todo-critical`:

   ```
   .todo {
     border: 2px solid black;
     text-align: center;
     background: $todo-normal;
     color: #333;
     margin: 20px;
     padding: 20px;
   }

   .done {
     background: $todo-complete;
   }

   .hr {
     border: 2px solid red;
   }

   .critical {
     composes: todo;
     background: $todo-critical;
   }
   ```

4. Save and reload our project, and let's make sure the new color scheme is being respected:

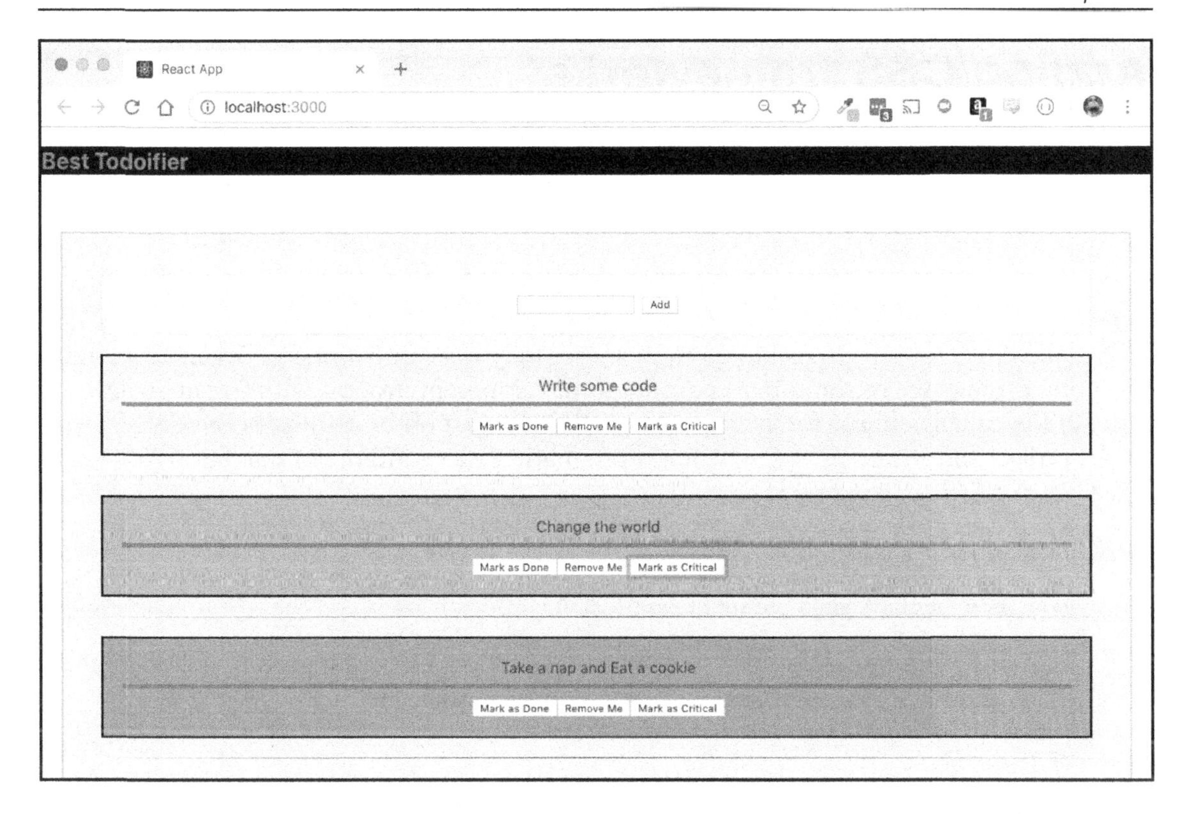

Honestly, everything beyond this point is just diving deeper and deeper into SASS-specific syntax, and again, that falls pretty far outside of the scope of this book. As you can see from the preceding screenshot though, we were able to introduce SASS into our CSS Modules code with no real complications.

Even better, we've now introduced a new way to change themes and skins in our project without a ton of extra work, and if our designers ever want to run in and change, for example, the backgrounds of all of the Todos and change the general color scheme, they can do so by running into the `shared.scss` file quickly and making a few color changes, and not having to change much else!

We can keep the lovely code modularity and developer-centric features of CSS Modules and SASS, but also provide nice inlets into our code to allow designers and other non-developers to modify the design and style elements where necessary! Even better, our code gets easier to maintain with the addition of two new features instead of making our project exponentially more complicated!

Adding CSS frameworks

A very common use case that you'll run into as part of working on a frontend project is integrating some sort of third-party CSS framework. This is something I've had to do on nearly every frontend development project I've ever touched, and there's pretty good odds that you'll need to run through this same process!

We'll stick to one of the most common ones, since it will give you a good introduction to using frameworks in general, so we'll start off by integrating bootstrap into our project! It won't take much for our project to go from sort of ugly to actually kind of decent! As with most other things we've run into as part of our development process with Create React App, this is equally simple for us to implement! We'll start off by adding both `bootstrap` to our project and `reactstrap`, which is a pre-made React component that takes full advantage of Twitter Bootstrap!

We'll start by adding `bootstrap`, and `reactstrap`, via `yarn`:

```
$ yarn add bootstrap@4 reactstrap@6.5.0
```

Right now, if you use `bootstrap` at version 4.x, you'll need to include `reactstrap`, but at 6.5.x to avoid error messages!

We should see a bunch of things get installed in our project folder, but hopefully no errors! After everything is successfully installed, we can then get the baseline `bootstrap` into our project by opening up `src/index.js` and adding a single `import` statement:

```
import 'bootstrap/dist/css/bootstrap.css';
```

Cleaning up our design, starting with the header

Next, let's clean up our ugly header, which will also require us to remove some of the code we wrote earlier to experiment with JavaScript syntax! Currently, our `header` is our own pre-rolled thing but it's not very good-looking as it is right now. We'll want to take advantage of the `Navbar` and `NavbarBrand` components that `reactstrap` provides to us as part of its standard exports! Open up `src/App/App.js`, and we're going to start modifying the file pretty significantly:

1. We'll start off by adding our `Navbar` and `NavbarBrand` imports at the top:

```
import { Navbar, NavbarBrand } from "reactstrap";
```

2. Next, we can remove all of the `header` configuration objects, since we won't need any of them after we're done editing this file. Instead, we'll just replace it with a single `headerTitle` variable:

```
const headerTitle = "Todoifier";
```

3. Next, we'll need to replace our `headerDisplay` function, since it is going to be using the new `reactstrap` component instead of the previous code we had in place:

```
const headerDisplay = (title) => (
  <Navbar color="dark" dark expand="md">
    <NavbarBrand href="/">{title}</NavbarBrand>
  </Navbar>
);
```

Notice that, now, `header` only accepts a passed in title instead of the huge configuration object we were using earlier. This simplifies our code pretty significantly! We'll also need to change the call in our `App` component to our `header` function:

```
const App = () => (
  <div className="App">
    {headerDisplay(headerTitle)}
    <br />
    <TodoList />
  </div>
);
```

4. Save it and we should have a significantly cleaner `header` in our project! Refer to the following screenshot:

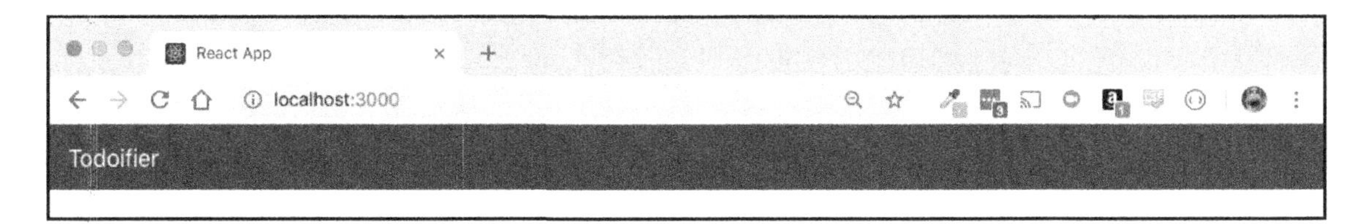

Cleaning up the NewTodo component

We'll also want to clean up our `NewTodo` component, since it is pretty bare bones right now! We'll basically want to update anywhere a `Button` or `Input` function appears in our code to make sure our app has a clean, consistent design all over the place!

1. First, at the top of `src/NewTodo/NewTodo.js`, we'll want to add our `reactstrap` imports! We'll need `Button`, `Input`, and `InputGroup`, so let's add them as our named imports from `reactstrap`:

```
import { Button, Input, InputGroup } from "reactstrap";
```

2. Next, we'll need to clean up the text `Input` and `Button` display properly, so let's wrap our text field and `Button` inside of an `InputGroup` component to keep them together! We'll change the text `Input` to the `reactstrap Input` component and the `Button` tag to a `reactstrap Button` component as well, and we'll add a `placeholder` text for our input item. Also, note that we're setting a new property on our `Button` tag called `color`, which is set to `"primary"`. This gives us a blue button instead of the default ugly grey button! Our `render()` function should now look like this:

```
render() {
  return (
    <div className="NewTodo">
      <InputGroup>
        <Input
          type="text"
          onChange={this.handleUpdate}
          value={this.state.item}
          placeholder="Input item name here..."
        />
        <Button onClick={this.addTodo}
        color="primary">Add</Button>
      </InputGroup>
    </div>
  );
}
```

3. Save and reload, and our input should look much nicer; something like the following:

Cleaning up our Todo component

Our `Todo` components still look a little ugly, so let's also give them the same treatment. After this, we'll be in a good enough place to call it quits with making our project look a little nicer, but to get there we'll need some more imports:

1. We'll need to `import`, `Button`, and `ButtonGroup` to our `Todo` components, since the only things we'll want to clean up are our buttons! To do so, use the following code, adding it to `src/Todo/Todo.js`:

```
import { Button, ButtonGroup } from "reactstrap";
```

2. Next, hop right on down to the `render()` function in `src/Todo/Todo.js`, where we'll wrap our buttons inside of a `ButtonGroup` component, and change each of the `button` tags to `Button` components:

```
render() {
  return (
    <div className={this.cssClasses()}>
      {this.props.description}
      <br />
      <hr className={styles.hr} />
      <ButtonGroup>
        <Button className="MarkDone" onClick={this.markAsDone}
        color="success">
          Mark as Done
        </Button>
        <Button className="RemoveTodo" onClick={this.removeTodo}
        color="warning">
          Remove Me
        </Button>
        <Button className="MarkCritical"
```

```
onClick={this.markCritical}
            color="danger">
             Mark as Critical
           </Button>
         </ButtonGroup>
       </div>
     );
   }
```

3. Save and reload, and we should now see our project looking like this instead:

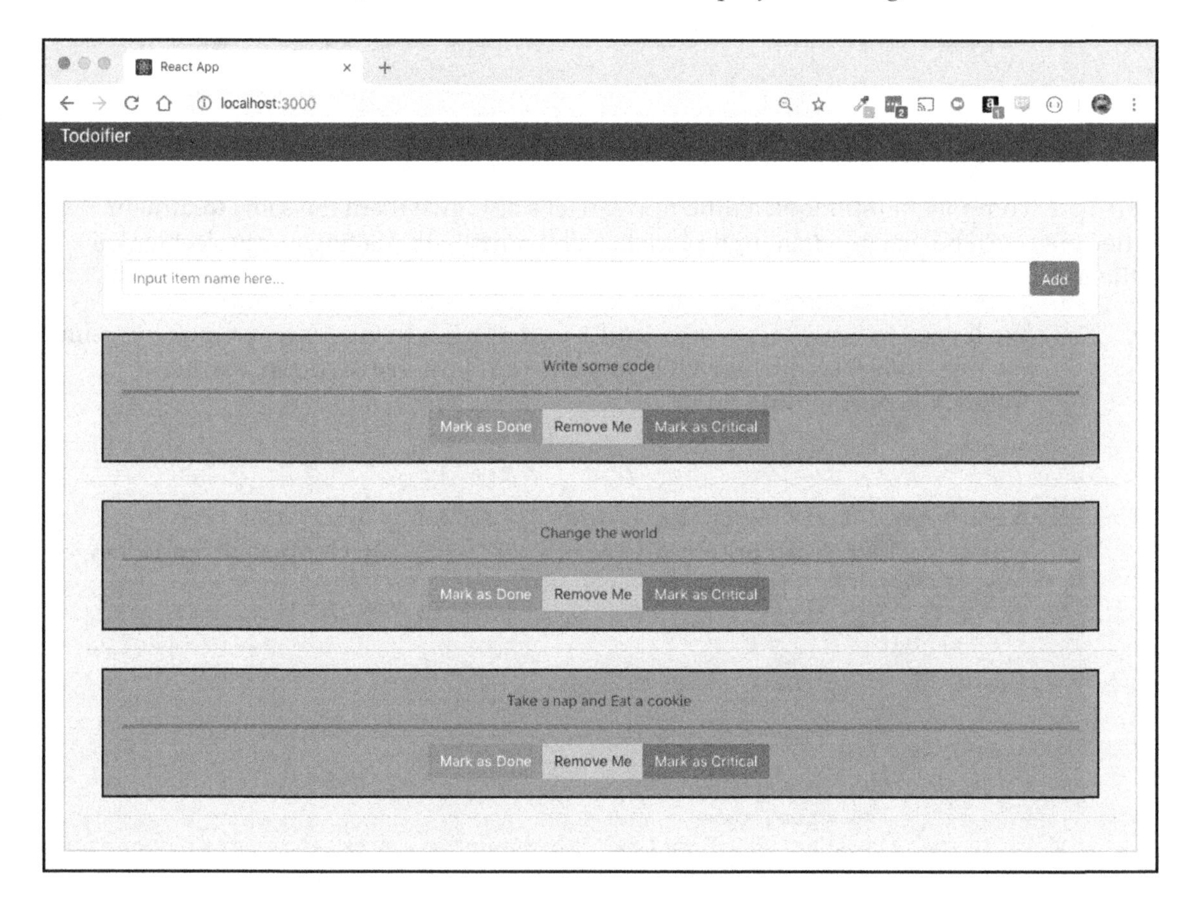

One thing we haven't fixed yet are our tests! We should now see a large number of failing tests, so we'll need to go in and fix them specifically!

Making our tests pass again

Since we've changed a bunch of `input` and `button` tags and we have tests that are specifically looking for them, we'll need to hop into `src/NewTodo/NewTodo.test.js` first, and change every instance of `.find("input")` and `.find("button")` to `.find("Input")`, and `.find("Button")`. We'll start with our first test, which tests the form:

```
it("contains the form", () => {
  expect(component.find("Input")).toHaveLength(1);
  expect(component.find("Button")).toHaveLength(1);
});
```

We'll also want to modify the next test that relies on simulating `button` clicks:

```
it("calls the passed in addTodo function when add button is clicked", ()
=> {
  component.find("Button").simulate("click");
  expect(mockAddTodo).toBeCalled();
});
```

We're almost done with this file! We have one more place where we're attempting to simulate a `button` click, so we'll need to clean up that test too! We can do this as follows:

```
it("blanks out the Todo Name when the button is clicked", () => {
  const updateKey = "I should be empty";
  component.instance().handleUpdate({ target: { value: updateKey } });
  expect(component.state("item")).toEqual(updateKey);
  component.find("Button").simulate("click");
  expect(component.state("item")).toHaveLength(0);
});
```

After saving and reloading, we should see fewer failed tests and can then move on to the next test suite that's failing! We can do this as follows:

```
FAIL src/Todo/Todo.test.js
 - Todo › marks the Todo as done

   Method "simulate" is meant to be run on 1 node. 0 found instead.

     34 |
     35 | it("marks the Todo as done", () => {
   > 36 | component.find("button.MarkDone").simulate("click");
        | ^
     37 | expect(component.state("done")).toEqual(true);
     38 | });
     39 |
```

```
      at ShallowWrapper.single
(node_modules/enzyme/build/ShallowWrapper.js:1875:17)
      at ShallowWrapper.simulate
(node_modules/enzyme/build/ShallowWrapper.js:1080:21)
      at Object.simulate (src/Todo/Todo.test.js:36:39)

  - Todo › calls the mock remove function

    Method "simulate" is meant to be run on 1 node. 0 found instead.

      39 |
      40 | it("calls the mock remove function", () => {
    > 41 | component.find("button.RemoveTodo").simulate("click");
         | ^
      42 | expect(mockRemoveTodo).toHaveBeenCalled();
      43 | });
      44 | });

      at ShallowWrapper.single
(node_modules/enzyme/build/ShallowWrapper.js:1875:17)
      at ShallowWrapper.simulate
(node_modules/enzyme/build/ShallowWrapper.js:1080:21)
      at Object.simulate (src/Todo/Todo.test.js:41:41)

 PASS src/TodoList/TodoList.test.js
 PASS src/App/App.test.js

Test Suites: 1 failed, 3 passed, 4 total
Tests: 2 failed, 19 passed, 21 total
```

From the previous code snippet, we can see that the other failing test suite is in `src/Todo/Todo.test.js`, so let's fix that up too in the same way! Scroll to the very bottom of the file and change the two failing tests that are looking for `button` tags instead of `Button` components:

```
it("marks the Todo as done", () => {
  component.find("Button.MarkDone").simulate("click");
  expect(component.state("done")).toEqual(true);
});

it("calls the mock remove function", () => {
  component.find("Button.RemoveTodo").simulate("click");
  expect(mockRemoveTodo).toHaveBeenCalled();
});
```

Save the file, and when the tests come back up (you may have to hit *U* to update the `Snapshots` as well, don't forget), we should see a fully green test suite again, as follows:

```
 PASS src/Todo/Todo.test.js
 PASS src/NewTodo/NewTodo.test.js
 PASS src/App/App.test.js
 PASS src/TodoList/TodoList.test.js

Test Suites: 4 passed, 4 total
Tests: 21 passed, 21 total
Snapshots: 3 passed, 3 total
Time: 4.386s
Ran all test suites.

Watch Usage: Press w to show more.
```

We're *almost* there, but remember the new functionality that we added to our project to mark certain `Todo` items as `critical`? We never added new tests for it! The good news is that there's only one more test we need to write for it!

This test should be almost identical to the test for seeing when `Todo` items are clicked and marked as done; except, this time, we're looking for the `Mark Critical` button, where we'll simulate a click on that button. After the button is clicked, we should expect to see the `critical` property on the `state` of the `component` change from `false` to `true`, which also means we'll start off with a sanity check in our test to make sure the `critical` property starts off `false` *before* we click on the button, and ends as `true` after the button click! This is as follows:

```
it("marks the Todo as critical", () => {
expect(component.state("critical")).toEqual(false);
component.find("Button.MarkCritical").simulate("click");
expect(component.state("critical")).toEqual(true);
});
```

Get into the habit of writing these sanity checks in your tests, as they will help you avoid writing tests that mistakenly assume default states and lead to useless tests in the future!

That's it! Our design is clean, our test suite is green, and our project is moving forward at an awesome pace! We'll rerun our test suite again just to make sure that everything is still green, but if it is, then we can safely move on to the next challenge:

```
 PASS src/NewTodo/NewTodo.test.js
 PASS src/TodoList/TodoList.test.js
 PASS src/Todo/Todo.test.js
```

```
 PASS src/App/App.test.js

Test Suites: 4 passed, 4 total
Tests: 22 passed, 22 total
Snapshots: 3 passed, 3 total
Time: 4.969s
Ran all test suites.

Watch Usage: Press w to show more.
```

Summary

We've added some nice new functionality to our project but didn't really have to engage in a lot of the headache and setup (and heartache, I suppose) that comes with adding two new CSS processors to our project! We have CSS Modules and SASS playing nicely in our Create React App project and have had to install a single new dependency. We have them playing nicely *together* even, which is an even greater achievement!

We've cleaned up our code a little bit and started grouping things together, and introduced concepts such as shared SASS files to store variables for colors and values, which allows us to change a color, for example, in one place and have it affect everywhere the variable appears!

Our code is cleaner, our designer is happy, we're happy, and we can continue to push forward on our project without having to slow down. We've never had to dive into configuration files, or do anything much more complicated than installing a dependency! This is yet another massive win in favor of Create React App!

In the next chapter, we'll dive into how to build a simulated backend to your frontend project via Create React App's incredibly nice proxy API functionality!

6 Simulate Your Backend with a Proxy API

As we've been working through building up our application, we've done a ton of really great work but nearly all of it has been in this weird state where the data all lives completely inside of our React application. The reality is that this won't be true for most projects you work on, so we'll want to do a little bit of work to try to put the state of our Create React App project outside of React itself. To do that, we can take advantage of another feature in our Create React App world: proxy backends!

In addition, we'll need to spend a little bit of time talking about how we can actually get the data from that backend server into our Create React App project! A backend without a frontend isn't particularly useful, and vice versa! Similarly, a developer who has no understanding of either direction will be in a difficult situation, where they are designing systems with no sense of how they would need to interact with each other!

The simulated backend server we'll be building will act as the design document for our frontend developers to follow. It's not meant to be the final backend that we'll actually use, but rather, it will function as the framework that other developers can work with to better understand how to properly interact with our frontend and how to build a backend API that doesn't require us to completely rebuild our frontend!

In this chapter, we will cover the following topics:

- Learning about the proxy feature
- Implementing a quick `Express.js` server that should have a small footprint
- Learning a little bit about the React component methods
- Getting data in or out of our backend proxy via Fetch
- Updating our tests

Simulating a backend server with the proxy API

We've been building up our application over time with Create React App, but we've kept it almost entirely a frontend-only application. That's all well and good, but the reality is that you will probably be building an application that has a server behind it! The good news is that creating a simulated backend in Create React App projects remains as simple as possible while still giving you a good feel for how things would translate into a real-world scenario or project!

Setting up the backend API

As mentioned, pretending there is a backend to our Create React App project requires very little effort and gets us back into development incredibly quickly. For us to take advantage of this, we'll need to first set up a `"proxy"` in our `package.json` file. A proxy is a way for us to tell Create React App that any requests we make should go to this other server when it may look like we're making requests locally, instead. Let's start with configuring our project and then move on to implementing this further:

```
"proxy": "http://localhost:4000"
```

We'll also want to add a command to run and execute our server that we can easily run via `yarn`, so we'll also need to update the `"scripts"` section of `package.json` to include a new command. We'll arbitrarily name it `"backend"` so that when we're ready to run our server, we just run the `yarn backend` command:

```
"scripts": {
  "start": "react-scripts start",
  "build": "react-scripts build",
  "test": "react-scripts test",
  "eject": "react-scripts eject",
  "backend": "node server.js"
},
```

This by itself won't actually do anything. We'll need to implement a `server` behind the scenes that can actually respond and react to any of the API calls that we're making along the way. We'll need another library in our project to do that, though, since by itself we can't just simulate an API. We'll need to add another library to our project that can handle the server and `HTTP` functionality. I personally prefer using `Express.js` for this, so we'll use that as our library of choice for this project. In our command window, we'll add express via `yarn`:

```
$ yarn add express
```

We then create a new file in the root of our Create React App project called `server.js`. This will act as the code that will serve all of the the requests that our application will be making to simulate a real-world scenario. Our server will not actually be stateful; instead, we will simulate that behavior through static data returned from our little, fake API.

This section is going to be a little heavier on Node.js and Express concepts than React, since we need to be able to set up a quick server to act as our simulated backend!

We'll start off with a basic skeleton for our server, which will do a little bit of setup work that `express` requires from us. In `server.js`, in our root directory of our project, we will have the following:

```
const express = require('express');
const app = express();
const port = 4000;

app.use(express.json());

app.get('/', (req, res) => res.json({}));

app.listen(port, () =>
  console.log(`Simulated backend listening on port ${port}!`)
);
```

We'll start off by loading Express into our server project. We'll need to pull this into our project via a `require()` statement rather than an `import()` statement, since we will be running this via Node. Next, we'll need to build out our server in our app variable, which is the instantiation of the `express.js` code. We'll also set the port that we'll run this on, which is the port we specified in our proxy configuration. I tend to pick ports in multiples of 1,000, but you can use whatever port numbers you personally prefer!

Next, we'll need to tell our app to use the express JSON middleware, which will let us react and respond to JSON post body statements later on (we'll need this when we go to create a new `Todo` item in our server). After that, we have our first example of a route in our express server. This just returns, in JSON, an empty body when someone makes a request to the root of our proxy API backend.

Let's spend a few minutes talking a little bit more about the structure of a route in express. While we won't get into the full details and write the whole thing out from start to finish, it is worth at least understanding what a route is and how it is written in Express to avoid any confusion later on.

A route is structured and written as `(the name of the express() variable).(HTTP method)("path", (request_variable, response_variable)` and then a function off of that. Every route should end with sending something back to the requester, and, in our case (since we're writing a little API), it should be sending back some JSON.

This is enough for us to do right now; we'll be expanding on this configuration later on in this chapter!

Middleware is a pipeline of functions that are executed in between the time the server sees the request, the request goes into the proper route, and then is returned back to the sender. In this case, all JSON bodies are converted into JSON so that we can read from them without a lot of extra code each time.

Finally, we'll need to set up a listener for our application. We'll listen to the port that we specified earlier, and then specify a function that is to be executed when the app finishes listening on that port. In our case, we'll just have a little message that logs out letting us know that the server is set up and running correctly!

This code is very minimal, but as a result of how minimal it is, it also requires some maintenance. For example, every time you make a change in the code, you will need to restart your backend server (not the Create React App project, though).

Figuring out our backend requests

To figure out how we'll need to structure our API, it helps to take another look at the UI to identify different types of functions that can occur:

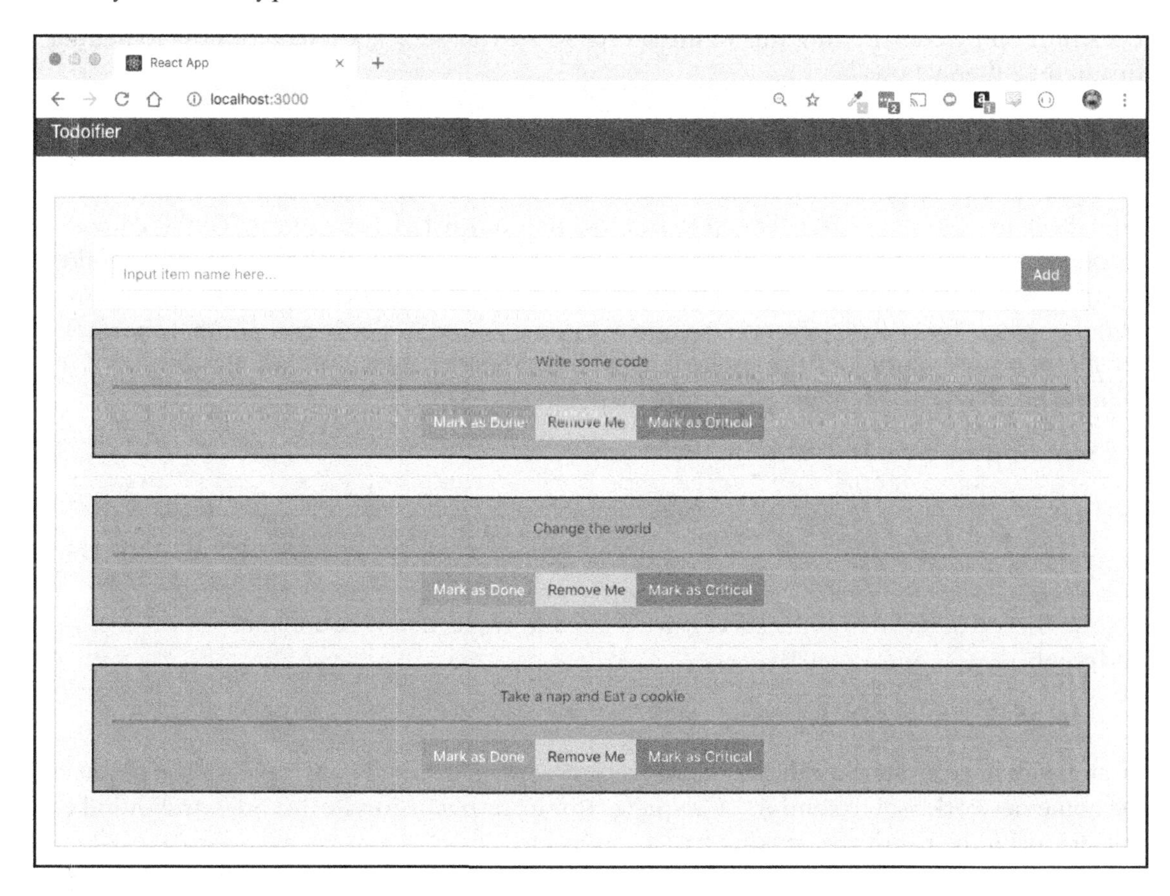

Looking at that UI, can you figure out what we need? We need representations of `Todo` items and a way to get the current list of them, and we need a way to change their state, to delete items, or to add new items. We'll start off simple by implementing our index of Todos, but that will require an initial step of figuring out the data structure we're going to use. First, we'll need an object for each `todo`. Each `todo` will need the same representation as their internal objects:

```
{ description: String, done: Boolean, critical: Boolean }
```

We'll also need a representation of some instances of internal `id`, so our new object would be as follows:

```
{ id: Number, description: String, done: Boolean, critical: Boolean }
```

Let's start off by constructing this in the server so we can get a good feel for how to handle this in the other actions later!

Building the Todos index API request

First, back in `server.js`, we'll need to put together our list of `Todo` items. You'll likely recognize these from the `Todo` items that we've used previously, with the exception of the fact that we now also have some `id` in the items as well. This is a closer representation to what we'd see normally in a server, where the items would not only contain their normal attributes but also form of primary keys as well. We'll store these as a `const` since we don't want to be able to accidentally overwrite them later:

```
const todos = [
  { id: 1, description: 'Write some code', done: false, critical: false },
  { id: 2, description: 'Change the world', done: false, critical: false },
  { id: 3, description: 'Eat a cookie', done: false, critical: false }
];
```

To `get` these Todos out via the server, we'll need to create a new route to an endpoint, `/api/todos`:

```
app.get('/api/todos', (req, res) => res.json({ todos: todos }));
```

First, you'll need to start up the backend using `yarn backend`. Next, if we send a request via some network tool to send `HTTP` requests (for example, using Postman), we should be able to verify the results by making a `GET` request to `http://localhost:4000/api/todos`:

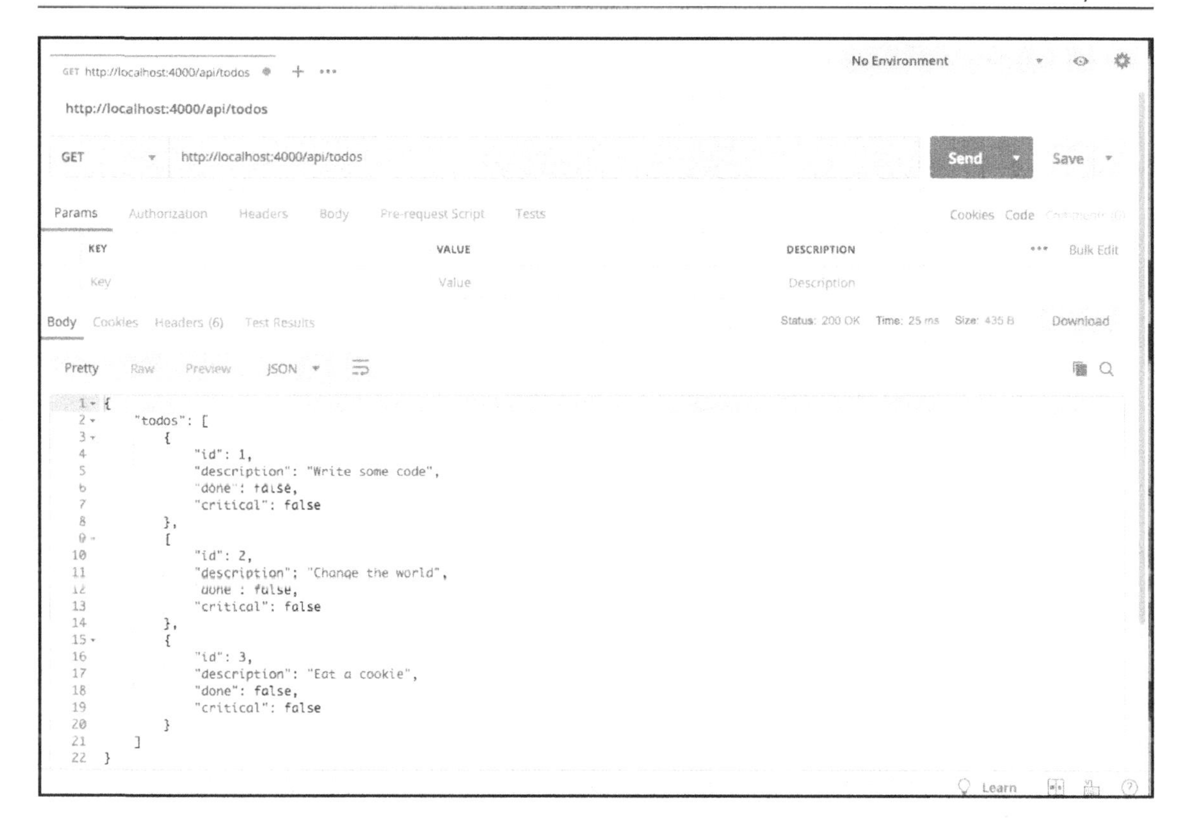

We can also delete the `app.get("/"...)` line, since we no longer require that code.

There are a lot of ways to simulate requests to your backend. Similar to choices on code editors, Postman is my tool of choice for manually sending `HTTP` requests to verify the results, or you may already have tools available to you, such as CURL! Whatever you prefer to use should work just fine.

Building the add Todo API request

We'll also need to be able to create new Todos. To do that, we'll implement the next portion of our API, where we will create a route in `server.js` that is able to handle receiving an `HTTP` post with a body. Remember that line of code from earlier, where we instructed express to use the JSON middleware? The code for this isn't very complicated either. We specify to express that we can accept an `HTTP` post and give it the standard `req`, `res` arguments.

From there, since we only have a few items in our `Todo` list, we give the new `Todo` an `id` of the length of that list plus one, and then we fill it up with the rest of the body that is passed in by the user, using the object spread operator! As follows:

```
app.post("/api/todos", (req, res) => {
  const body = { id: todos.length + 1, ...req.body };
  res.json({ todos: [...todos, body] });
});
```

Again, to verify that we're doing things correctly, we'll send a quick test via Postman with a `Todo` body and verify that we get sent back the list of Todos, plus the new one that we post in! Refer to the following screenshot:

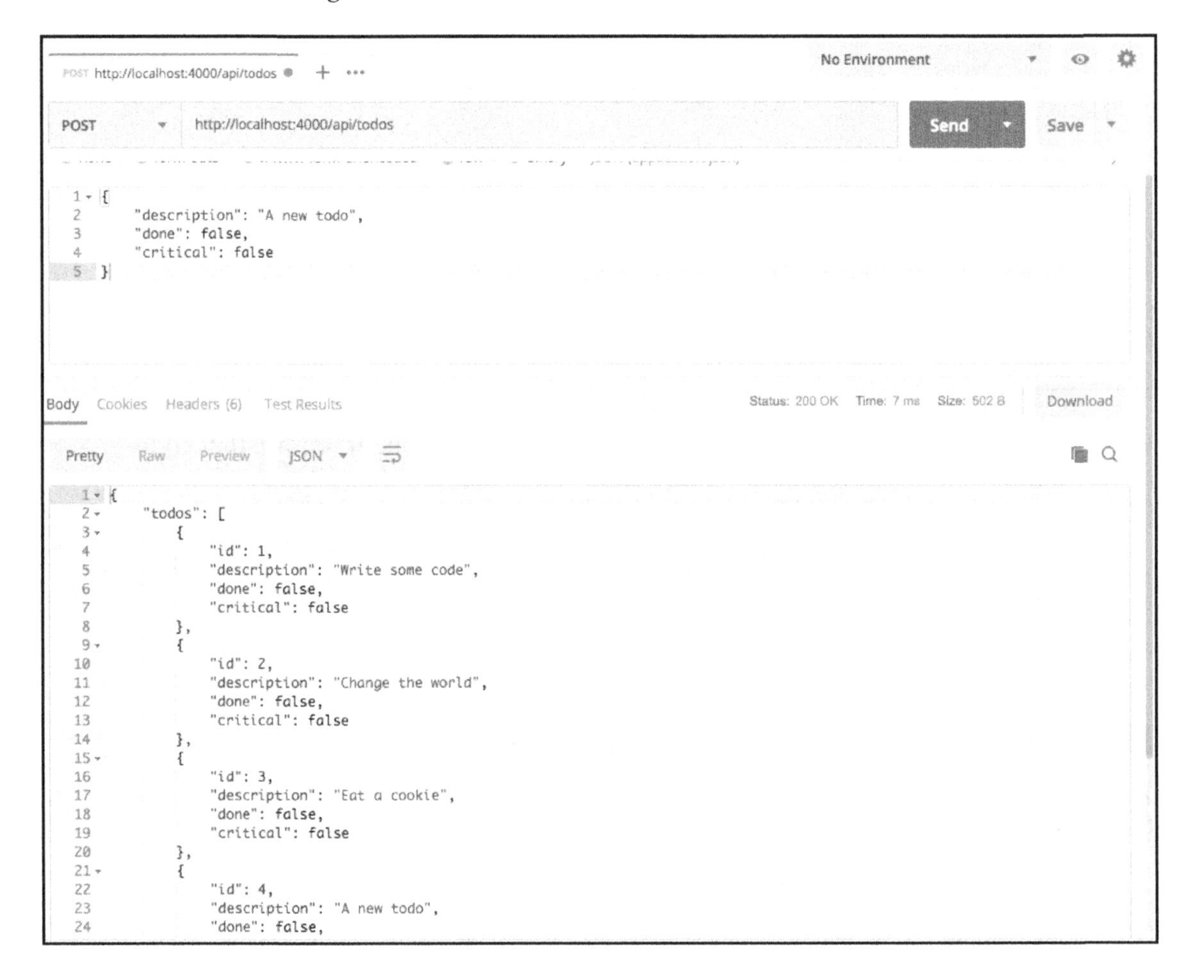

That's all we need to add a new `Todo`, so now we can move on to the next piece of functionality: deleting a `Todo`!

Building the remove Todo API request

Deleting a `Todo` is equally simple! Much like accepting a post route, we have to accept a delete route and specify an `id` in the body. This will allow us to use a URL such as `/api/todos/3`, where `3` would be the `id` of the `Todo` we want to delete! We can access `params` in the URL via `req.params.[the name of the param]`. In the following case, the name of the param we specify is `:id`, which means the variable we can access is `req.params.id`!

From there, we just `filter` out the instances of `id` that don't match and call it a day! Remember that any `params` URLs are passed in as strings; that's why we do a quick `parseInt()` on the `id` before our `filter` function! As follows:

```
app.delete("/api/todos/:id", (req, res) => {
  const todoId = parseInt(req.params.id);
  res.json({ todos: todos.filter(t => t.id !== todoId) });
});
```

Then we'll run it in Postman and verify the results:

The React component life cycle for mounting

We need to understand the React component life cycle for mounting components as well, since we'll need to hook into that later as part of hooking everything back up to our application. There are two main categories of phases when dealing with React components. The first is the **Render Phase**, where React is concerned about how the initial component is created and rendered to the page. You should keep these clean and without side-effects, so, as an example, we would not include any calls to our backend to fill in data or components on the page. The functions that are most commonly used here are `constructor()` and `render()`.

The second phase, however, is the phase where we can modify things after the fact. The main function to mention here is `componentDidMount()`, which is where we can (and will) fire off requests to our backend server. The diagram for these calls might look something like this:

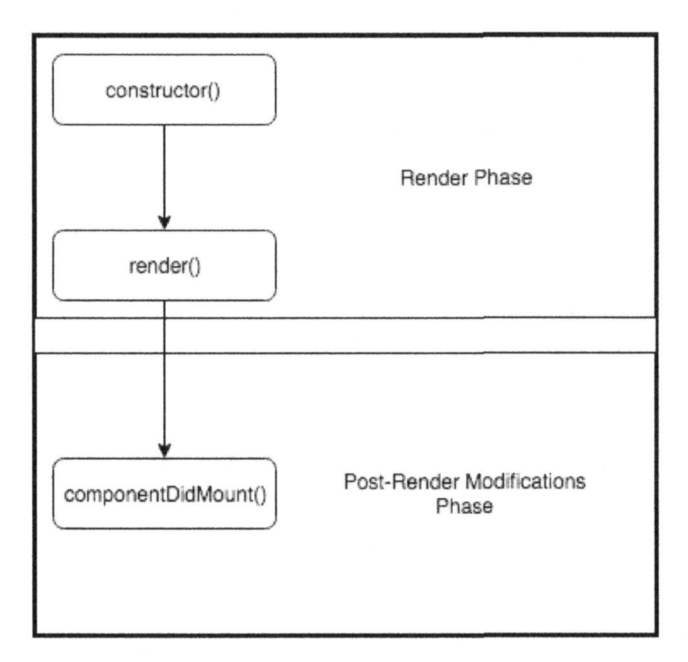

Where to put API requests

Based on that, we will have to create a `componentDidMount()` function that will contain the code that we need to fire off requests to our backend server, instead of sticking them in `constructor()` or in some other function! This ensures that our component will update and mount in a sane manner!

Communicating with your proxy server with React

Now that we've written all of the code that we need for now on the server side of things, we'll need to modify our `TodoList` component to actually make calls out to the service that we wrote! The great news is that, yet again, everything we need to be able to do this already exists for us in our Create React App project!

This is also a good opportunity for us to talk about another modern Javascript function: `Async/Await`!

Working with Async/Await

If we want to fetch data out of the server, the best tool for us to do that is by using some new Javascript syntax around asynchronous actions and calls!

This is called `Async/Await`, and is a method of performing operations that don't require our application to completely hang, but will wait for results while processing other data. If you're familiar with promises, you might be familiar with code that looks something like this:

```
doSomethingAsync().then(doSomething()).then(doSomethingElse())
```

This is fine, but there is a better way to do this. This code can get particularly messy the larger it grows, and even more so if we introduce different branches or failure criteria and conditions we need to account for. Eventually, a mess of promises can turn into code that is just impossible to trace through when things go wrong, and we want to avoid that if we can.

Introducing Fetch

The good news is that Fetch is also an incredibly simple library to work with! The syntax for it is simple and clear enough that it should be easy to understand what it does pretty quickly. Of course, that begs the question: what is Fetch?

The short answer is that Fetch is an `HTTP` request mechanism that has been made a first-class citizen in the Javascript world. The long answer is that Fetch is an attempt by the Javascript community and contributors to handle `HTTP` requests from Javascript code in a standardized way, instead of the multiple hundreds (or maybe even thousands) of different choices that all require their own implementations, patterns, configurations, and so on.

Fetch's utility stems from it being ubiquitous and part of the Javascript language standard, although not every browser supports it fully yet. As such, instead of picking some other random library to work with, it is much easier for us to rely instead on the standard, knowing full well that the skills learned as you work with Fetch should transfer just fine into any other libraries that you might pick up and start using.

Getting our list of Todos from the server

To get Todos, we'll need to change how our state is built out. If you think back to our earliest implementations of the `TodoList` component, we built all of our Todos as an array of strings and then allowed our `Todo` component to do the rest of the work. This ends up not being a great model when we're actually getting information in and out of our server, so we'll want to transition ourselves over from relying on simple strings to store the information about the Todos to a model where the data structures for the Todos match both their component implementations and their data representations on the server side.

To start modifying `TodoList` to fit our new world, we'll want to start with a blank list of Todos and a flag to capture whether the data has been loaded yet or not. In `src/TodoList/TodoList.js` add the following code:

```
constructor(props) {
  super(props);

  this.state = {
    items: [],
    loaded: false
  };

  this.addTodo = this.addTodo.bind(this);
  this.removeTodo = this.removeTodo.bind(this);
}
```

This `loaded` flag is actually pretty important; without it, we run into a scenario where when the page first loads, either the page looks blank or it displays *No items*, when in reality it just hasn't loaded the full list of items yet! To create a better user experience, we'll instead want to rely on a flag that tells the application whether it has completed loading and displays a message about that to the user, instead of relying on whether the `items state` property has values in it.

If you remember from our server, `Todo` items will now be populated from the data structure that we created in our server file, so they can no longer just be the descriptions. This will require us to restructure some of our code, so we'll go back through and fix up the code that is broken by this change. First, let's add a new item:

```
addTodo(description) {
  const newItem = {
    description: description,
    done: false,
    critical: false
  };
  this.setState({
    items: [...this.state.items, newItem]
  });
}
```

It's easier for us to break `newItem` into a separate variable and then pass that into the `setState()` call, otherwise we'd end up making that line of code really long and also very fragile in regards to any data-structure changes that might happen along the way:

```
removeTodo(removeItem) {
  const filteredItems = this.state.items.filter(todo => {
    return todo.description !== removeItem;
  });
  this.setState({ items: filteredItems });
}
```

We also do a similar operation with our `removeTodo` call. We'll move our list of filtered items, based on the description. Next, is our `renderItems()` call, which is also going to check the new state variable to see whether the data has been loaded from the server yet. Also, we're going to pass in a few new properties to our `Todo` component to make it respect our data structure. Specifically, we'll pass in the `id`, `done`, and `critical` flags to allow those to be set in `Todo` as part of the passed-in `props`:

```
renderItems() {
  if (this.state.loaded) {
    return this.state.items.map(todo => (
      <Fragment key={'item-' + todo.description}>
```

```
          <Todo
            id={todo.id}
            key={todo.id}
            description={todo.description}
            removeTodo={this.removeTodo}
            done={todo.done}
            critical={todo.critical}
          />
          <Divider key={'divide-' + todo.description} />
        </Fragment>
      ));
    } else {
      return <p>Still Loading...</p>;
    }
  }
```

Note that we're passing in some new props to the `Todo` components, which means we'll need to modify those to allow `state` to be set via `props` for whether a `Todo` is done and whether a `Todo` is critical. Open up `src/Todo/Todo.js` and we'll take care of that really quickly in the `constructor()` function:

```
  constructor(props) {
    super(props);
    this.state = {
      done: props.done,
      critical: props.critical
    };

    this.markAsDone = this.markAsDone.bind(this);
    this.removeTodo = this.removeTodo.bind(this);
    this.markCritical = this.markCritical.bind(this);
  }
```

Head back to `src/TodoList/TodoList.js`, and let's start writing our `Async/Await` functionality. We'll create a new function that is part of the React standard component life cycle, `componentDidMount()`, where we will declare it as an `async` function. Remember that any place we want to use `await` in our code, we have to do so inside of a function that has been declared as `async`! We'll start off with a simple body so that we can verify how it all works first, and then we'll flesh it out a little more:

```
  async componentDidMount() {
    this.setState({ loaded: true });
  }
```

Next, we'll need to use `fetch` to make the request to our simulated backend, where we will `await` the results of `fetch`:

```
const res = await fetch('/api/todos', { accept: 'application/json' });
```

Remember that we are proxying requests to a different backend through Create React App! As a result, we don't need to specify a port or host, since it is pretending to be the same port/host.

This backend server is meant to act as a placeholder for when you build a backend onto the same application or service as where this code runs for minimum latency. This is a great model for when you're building the frontend for something but the backend isn't fully built yet!

We'll also need to take those results and convert them into JSON if we want to do anything with them, which is also an `async` call:

```
const json = await res.json();
```

Finally, don't forget that our server returns data back in the following form:

```
{
  todos: [ ...todo1, ...todo2, ...etc ]
}
```

So finally, we need to replace the state of items to the new state:

```
this.setState({ items: json.todos, loaded: true });
```

And there we are! Now when the page refreshes, you should see the same list of components as before but now the data comes from our simulated backend instead! This should leave the full body of this function looking like the following code snippet:

```
async componentDidMount() {
  const res = await fetch('/api/todos', { accept: 'application/json' });
  const json = await res.json();
  this.setState({ items: json.todos, loaded: true });
}
```

Creating a new Todo on the server

We'll also want to be able to create a new `Todo` by using `HTTP` post to create a new `Todo`. This will also be an `async` function since we'll be making an `async` call to `fetch` to send data. Since posting via `HTTP` is more complicated than getting, we'll also need to specify some options into our `fetch` call. Specifically, we can configure the call by specifying the `HTTP` method (`POST` in our case), the headers (just an accept `header` for JSON data, which is the same as what we'd normally use to communicate with any JSON API), and the body of what we're posting to the server, which is just the data structure of a new `Todo`. If it is successful, we will add the new `Todo` onto our state and call it a day. Back in `src/TodoList/TodoList.js`, as follows:

```
async addTodo(description) {
  const res = await fetch('/api/todos', {
    method: 'POST',
    headers: { accept: 'application/json', 'content-type':
'application/json'  },
    body: JSON.stringify({ description: description, critical: false,
done: false })
  });
  if (res.status === 200) {
    const newItem = {
      id: this.state.items.length + 1,
      description: description,
      done: false,
      critical: false
    };
    this.setState({
      items: [...this.state.items, newItem]
    });
  }
}
```

Deleting a Todo

Deleting a `Todo` is going to be very similar to creating a `Todo`, so there's not actually that much that we have to describe here. The biggest and most important things are that the method is set to `DELETE` and the `id` of the `Todo` we want to delete is passed in via the URL:

```
async removeTodo(removeItemId) {
  const res = await fetch(`/api/todos/${removeItemId}`, {
    method: 'DELETE',
    headers: { accept: 'application/json', 'content-type':
'application/json' }
```

```
    });
    if (res.status === 200) {
      const filteredItems = this.state.items.filter(todo => {
        return todo.id !== removeItemId;
      });
      this.setState({ items: filteredItems });
    }
  }
```

We'll also need to change how the `removeTodo` function is called from `src/Todo/Todo.js`, so open that file up and change the argument that it passes in to be by the Todo's `id` instead of by its description! As follows:

```
removeTodo() {
  this.props.removeTodo(this.props.id);
}
```

This should get us most of the functionality that we want, but the problem we have right now is that our code is not nearly as simple to test as we'd like. In fact, we actually have a few failing tests that we'll need to fix up!

Getting back to passing tests

Tests are failing. We'll start by hitting *u* to update our snapshots, then move on to working with our code to fix up the rest of the tests. The good news is that our tests for the `Todo` component are really easy to fix up! Remember that our `Todo` component takes in a few other properties to initialize now; as per our test, it really only takes in the `description` and `removeTodo` properties.

Fixing the Todo test

We need to change our initialization of the shallow-rendered component to take in the `id`, `critical`, and `done` properties instead! In `src/Todo/Todo.test.js`, we'll change the first failing test suite by changing the `const component` statement to include these additional properties:

```
const component = shallow(
  <Todo
    description={description}
    removeTodo={mockRemoveTodo}
    critical={false}
    done={false}
    id={1}
```

```
    />
  );
```

Rerun the tests and now we should only be down to a single failing test suite! Unfortunately, this will also be the hardest test suite to fix!

Fixing our last failing test suite through refactoring

Unfortunately, our code now brings us into a scenario where our components are actually really hard to test appropriately. We have the code that has to fetch data off the backend mixed in with the code that initializes our components, as well as being mixed in with the behaviors when buttons are clicked! That's no good, so we'll need to fix this!

The good news is that the easiest way for us to fix this up doesn't require a mountain of effort; instead, it requires us to just move some of the code around in a way that would make it more extensible. The first operation we'll need to perform is moving all of our code that interacts with the backend into its own separate service library!

The service library pattern is a great pattern for when you need to lock down behaviors and interactions with external services into simpler APIs that make it easier for your code, or other people's code, to interact efficiently with a backend server!

Building service libraries

We'll start off by moving all of our API calls into a new file, `src/TodoService.js`. We'll start with the simplest call, which is the call to `fetchTodos` items from the server:

```
const fetchTodos = async () => {
  const res = await fetch("/api/todos", { accept: "application/json" });
  const json = await res.json();
  return { status: res.status, todos: json.todos };
};
```

Here, we've written our `fetchTodos()` function as an `async` function that, for the most part, does what it did originally. The only major different here is that we've changed the `return` statement to not just send back the list of `todos` from the server, but also the `HTTP` status code from the server!

Next, we'll implement the call to create a `Todo` on the server:

```
const createTodo = async description => {
  const res = await fetch("/api/todos", {
    method: "POST",
    headers: { accept: "application/json" },
    body: JSON.stringify({
      description: description,
      critical: false,
      done: false
    })
  });
  const json = await res.json();
  return { status: res.status, todos: json.todos };
};
```

Again, this post is almost identical to what you saw previously, except with the modification around the `return` statement. Finally, we'll move on to the delete call on our server:

```
const deleteTodo = async todoId => {
  const res = await fetch(`/api/todos/${todoId}`, {
    method: "DELETE",
    headers: { accept: "application/json" }
  });
  const json = await res.json();
  return { status: res.status, todos: json.todos };
};
```

We've added a few functions, so we'll `export` them at the end of the service library. All we need to do is `export` these three functions as named functions:

```
export { fetchTodos, createTodo, deleteTodo };
```

Implementing our service library in TodoList

Now that we have our `TodoService` library, we have to go back to our `src/TodoList/TodoList.js` file and find all of the areas where we used to have the `fetch` code written into our component. We'll need to start off at the top of our file by importing those three named functions from our `TodoService`:

```
import { fetchTodos, createTodo, deleteTodo } from "../TodoService";
```

Next, we'll need to go into our `componentDidMount()` function, where we'll modify it to call the `fetchTodos()` function instead:

```
async componentDidMount() {
  const { todos } = await fetchTodos();
  this.setState({ items: todos, loaded: true });
}
```

Look at how nice and clean that function is now! This is definitely a move for the better, no matter what! Now, let's move on to our `addTodo()` function call:

```
async addTodo(description) {
  const { status } = await createTodo(description);
  if (status === 200) {
    const newItem = {
      id: this.state.items.length + 1,
      description: description,
      done: false,
      critical: false
    };
    this.setState({
      items: [...this.state.items, newItem]
    });
  }
}
```

Finally, we'll modify our `removeTodo()` function:

```
async removeTodo(todoId) {
  const { status } = await deleteTodo(todoId);
  if (status === 200) {
    const filteredItems = this.state.items.filter(todo => {
      return todo.id !== todoId;
    });
    this.setState({ items: filteredItems });
  }
}
```

This will get us most of the way back toward fixing our failing tests, but the last place we need to get some work done is in the failing tests themselves.

Finally fixing our last failing test suite

First, head on over to the failing test suite, `src/TodoList/TodoList.test.js`, where we will need to create something in Jest called a **mock library**. A mock library is basically just a way for us to tell Jest that we need to fake the behavior of a particular `import` module so that, whenever it is used, our fake mock functions will be used instead. This will allow us to mock the behavior of the entire service library that we wrote, allowing us to test our components and verify functionality without needing tests that actually make calls to some backend API somewhere!

We'll start the top of our test file, underneath our `import` statements, by adding the library mock and three `mock` functions:

```
jest.mock("../TodoService", () => ({
  fetchTodos: jest.fn().mockReturnValue({ status: 200, todos: [] }),
  createTodo: jest.fn().mockReturnValue({ status: 200, todos: [] }),
  deleteTodo: jest.fn().mockReturnValue({ status: 200, todos: [] })
}));
```

We're writing these in a way that the functions will always work, always return an empty list of `todos`, and will always return a fake `HTTP` status `200` code! With that out of the way, we can clean up our failing tests.

The two tests that are failing are doing so because the behavior is erratic when we're dealing with non-async tests that deal with `async` functionality! We can instead write our tests—similar to how we write the rest of our function calls—to be `async` functions! Think about the structure of a test declaration:

```
it("does some thing", () => {
  // Do some work here
});
```

If we wanted to instead make that test async-capable, we would instead write our test declaration as follows:

```
it("does some thing", async () => {
  // Do some work here
});
```

Bearing that in mind, let's take a look at the corrected function:

```
it("adds another Todo when the addTodo function is called", async () => {
  const before = component.find(Todo).length;
  await component.instance().addTodo("New Item");
  component.update();
  const after = component.find(Todo).length;
  expect(after).toBeGreaterThan(before);
});
```

It's not dramatically different from the test we had previously, with the addition of the call to `addTodo()` requiring an `await` statement. Now let's take a look at our test for `removeTodo()`:

```
 it("removes a Todo from the list when the remove Todo function is called",
async () => {
 const before = component.find(Todo).length;
 const removeMe = component.state("items")[0];
 await component.instance().removeTodo(removeMe.id);
 component.update();
 const after = component.find(Todo).length;
 expect(after).toBeLessThan(before);
 });
```

You might get an error message about the first test, the test where it tries to render a component without crashing. Our new `async/await` additions make this test no longer viable, so just delete it! Run the tests now, and we should see the follows:

```
 PASS src/Todo.test.js
 PASS src/App/App.test.js
 PASS src/TodoList/TodoList.test.js
 PASS src/NewTodo/NewTodo.test.js
 PASS src/Todo/Todo.test.js

Test Suites: 4 passed, 4 total
Tests: 21 passed, 21 total
Snapshots: 3 passed, 3 total
Time: 5.596s
Ran all test suites.
```

There we are, back to a fully-passing suite of tests!

Summary

In this chapter, we spent a fair amount of time exploring our options for making, simulating, and running a backend server alongside our Create React App project. This allows us to pass projects off to other teams where they know the implicit data structure contracts that need to exist as part of the development process between frontend and backend development teams.

We also spent a good chunk of time exploring our options for retrieving data from inside a React project out to a server! This is only one possible option for implementation out of many; in general, Javascript projects tend to have a ton of different (and all equally good in their own rights) ways to implement a lot of common functionality. Using Fetch and a service library is just one possible way to do this, but it's a way that I've personally found a lot of success with and tend to stick with, unless I see a need to do something more complicated.

In the next chapter, we'll explore some of the more progressive options for supporting a web application in a way that supports both mobile users and users with poor internet connections: progressive web apps! Create React App ships with really great support for building progressive web applications right out of the gate, so we'll take a deep dive into building a progressive web app, what functionality and opportunities that affords us, and how we can take advantage of that to make a truly modern React application, all while remaining inside the confines of our Create React App project!

7
Building Progressive Web Applications

The beauty of building a modern web application is being able to take advantage of functionalities such as a **Progressive Web App (PWA)**! But they can be a little complicated to work with. As always, the Create React App project makes a lot of this easier for us, but this time carries some significant caveats that we'll need to think about.

In this chapter, we will cover the following topics:

- Examining PWAs and what they add
- Learning how to configure our Create React App project into a custom PWA
- Modifying and tuning the `manifest` file
- Exploring service workers, their life cycle, and how to use them with Create React App
- Exploring the caveats of using Create React App to build a PWA

Understanding and building PWAs

PWAs are one of those features that sounds amazingly cool but it's surprisingly complicated to understand the when, why, and how of building them. Let's spend a little bit of time demystifying them and helping you understand why they are such a powerful (and appreciated) inclusion in our Create React App projects and how we can get started using them!

What is a PWA?

Let's talk a little bit about what a PWA is, because there is unfortunately a lot of misinformation and confusion about precisely what a PWA does!

Here's a short, maybe slightly unhelpful, version of what a PWA does; it's simply a website that does the following:

- Only uses `HTTPS`
- Adds a JSON manifest (a web app manifest) file
- Has a Service Worker

While yes, a PWA must have those behaviors, it's still difficult to understand what a PWA is or what it gives you in the long run. For example, does that tell you anything about what it does in different browsers? With different window sizes? What about how accessible it is, or how it functions when the internet is slow or non-existent?

How do we define a PWA?

A PWA, for us, is a React application that would be installable/runnable on a mobile device or desktop. Essentially, it's just your app, but with capabilities that make it a little more advanced, a little more effective, and a little more resilient to poor/no internet. A PWA accomplishes these via a few tenets, tricks, and requirements that we'd want to follow:

- The app must be usable by mobile and desktop-users alike
- The app must operate over `HTTPS`
- The app must implement a web app JSON `manifest` file
- The app must implement a Service Worker

Now, the first one is a design question. Did you make your design responsive? If so, congratulations, you built the first step toward having a PWA! The next one is also more of an implementation question that's maybe not as relevant to us here: when you deploy your app to production, did you make it `HTTPS` only? I hope the answer to this is yes, of course, but it's still a good question to ask!

The next two, though, are things we can do as part of our Create React App project, and we'll make those the focus of this chapter!

Building a PWA in Create React App

If we want to start building out a PWA in Create React App, as mentioned earlier, we need to start implementing against those two requirements that we laid out. We'll start off with the simplest problem to solve: implementing a `manifest` file for our PWA!

Starting with our manifest file

Okay, so I identified the two items that we need to build to make this all happen: the JSON `manifest` file and the service worker! Easy, right? Actually, it's even easier than that. You see, Create React App will populate a JSON `manifest` file for us as part of our project creation by default! That means we have already completed this step! Let's celebrate, go home, and kick off our shoes, because we're all done now, right?

Well, sort of. We should take a look at that default `manifest` file because it's very unlikely that we want our fancy `TodoList` project to be called `"Create React App Sample"`. Let's take a look at the `manifest` file, located in `public/manifest.json`:

```
{
 "short_name": "React App",
 "name": "Create React App Sample",
 "icons": [
 {
 "src": "favicon.ico",
 "sizes": "64x64 32x32 24x24 16x16",
 "type": "image/x-icon"
 }
 ],
 "start_url": ".",
 "display": "standalone",
 "theme_color": "#000000",
 "background_color": "#ffffff"
}
```

Some of these keys are pretty self-explanatory or at least have a little bit of information that you can infer from them as to what they accomplish. Some of the other keys, though, might be a little stranger. For example, what does `"start_url"` mean? What are the different options we can pick for display? What's a `"theme_color"` or `"background_color"`? Aren't those just decided by the CSS of our application?

Not quite. In fact, let's dive super deep into this world of JSON `manifest` files and turn it into something more useful!

Viewing our manifest file in action with Chrome

First, to be able to test this, we should have something where we can verify the results of our changes. We'll start off with Chrome, where if you go into the **Developer tools** section, you can navigate to the **Application** tab and be brought right to the **Service Workers** section! Let's take a look at what it all looks like for our application:

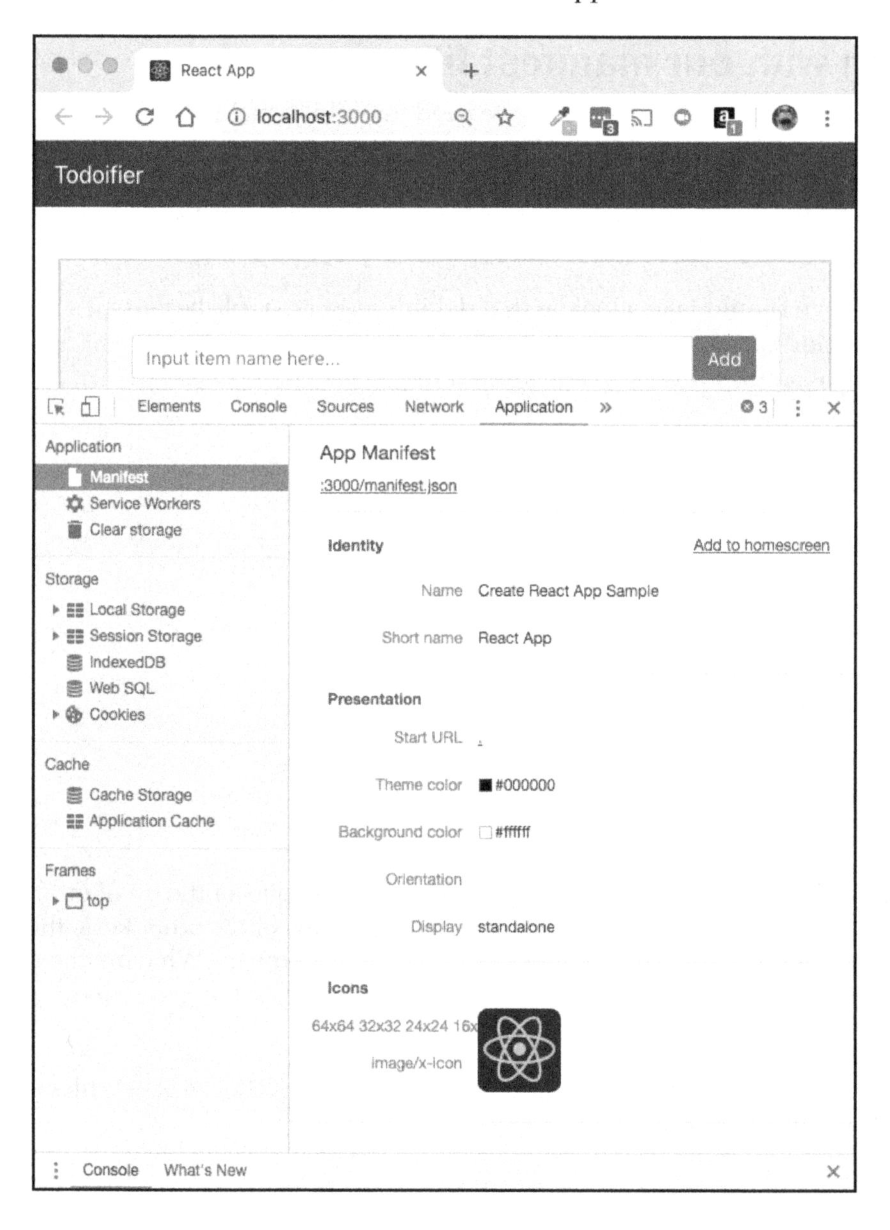

Exploring the manifest file options

Having a `manifest` file with no explanation of what the different keys and options mean is not very helpful, so let's take a deeper dive, key by key, into each of the configuration options available to us and some of the possible values we could use for each.

name and short_name

The first key we have is `short_name`. This is a shorter version of the name that might be displayed when, for example, the title can only display a smaller bit of text than the full app or site name. The counterpart to this is `name`, which is the full name of your application. A good example of this might be something like this:

```
{
 "short_name": "Todos",
 "name": "Best Todoifier"
}
```

icons

The next key to look at is the `"icons"` key, which is a list of sub-objects, each of which has three keys. This contains a list of icons that the PWA should use, whether it's for display on someone's desktop, someone's phone home screen, or something else. Each `"icon"` object should contain an `"src"`, which is a link to the image file that will be your icon. Next, you have the `"type"` key, which should tell the PWA what type of image file you're working with. For example, if you're using a `.png` file, you would list `"image/png"` here as the type. Finally, we have the `"sizes"` key, which tells the PWA the size of the icon. For best results, you should have at least a `"512x512"` and a `"192x192"` icon. The PWA will take care of scaling things down where necessary.

start_url

The `start_url` key is used to tell the application at what point it should start in your application in relation to your server. While we're not using it for anything as we have a single page, no route app, that might be different in a much larger application, so you might just want the `start_url` key to be something indicating where you want them to start off from. Another option would be to add a query string on to the end of `url`, such as a tracking link. An example of that would be something like this:

```
{
 "start_url": "/?source=AB12C"
}
```

background_color

This is the color used when a splash screen is displayed any time the application is first launched. This is similar to when you launch an application from your phone for the first time; that little page that pops up temporarily while the app loads is the splash screen, and this would be the background of that. This can either be a color name, like you'd use in CSS, or it can be a hex value for a color.

display

`display` affects the browser's UI when the application is launched. There are ways to make the application full-screen, to hide some of the UI elements, and so on. Here are the possible options, with their explanations:

`Value`	Description.
`browser`	A normal web browser experience.
`fullscreen`	No browser UI, and takes up the entire display.
`standalone`	Makes the web app look like a native application. It will run in its own window and hides a lot of the browser UI to make it look and feel more native.

For our example, we'll be using `standalone` as our setting for display!

orientation

If you want to make your application in the landscape orientation, you would specify it here. Otherwise you would leave this option missing from your `manifest`:

```
{
  "orientation": "landscape"
}
```

scope

Scope helps to determine where the PWA in your site lies and where it doesn't. This prevents your PWA from trying to load things outside where your PWA runs. `start_url` must be located inside your scope for it to work properly! This is optional, and in our case we'll be leaving it out.

theme_color

This sets the color of the tool bar, again to make it feel and look a little more native. If we specify a meta theme color, we'd set this to be the same as that specification. Much like background color, this can either be a color name, like you'd use in CSS, or it can be a hex value for a color.

Customizing our manifest file

Now that we're experts on `manifest` files, let's customize our manifest file! We're going to change a few things here and there, but we won't make any major changes. For the purposes of this book, we're not going to worry about working with the images, so we'll leave those be for now. Let's take a look at how we've set up the `manifest` file in `public/manifest.json`:

```
{
 "short_name": "Todos",
 "name": "Best Todoifier",
 "icons": [
 {
 "src": "favicon.ico",
 "sizes": "64x64 32x32 24x24 16x16",
 "type": "image/x-icon"
 }
 ],
 "start_url": "/",
 "display": "standalone",
 "theme_color": "#343a40",
 "background_color": "#a5a5f5"
}
```

So we've set our `short_name` and `name` keys to match the actual application. We've left the `icons` key alone completely since we don't really need to do much of anything with that anyway.

Next, we've changed `start_url` to just be `"/"`, since we're working under the assumption that this application is the only thing running on its domain. We've set the `display` to `standalone`, since we want our application to have the ability to be added to someone's home screen and be recognized as a true PWA.

Finally, we set the theme color to `#343a40`, which matches the color of the nav bar and will give a more seamless look and feel to the PWA. We also set the `background_color` key, which is for our splash screen, to `#a5a5f5`, which is the color of our normal `Todo` items!

If you think back to the explanation of keys, you'll remember we also need to change our meta theme tag in our `public/index.html` file, so we'll open that up and quickly make that change:

```
<meta name="theme-color" content="#343a40" />
```

And that's it! Our `manifest` file has been customized! If we did it all correctly, we should be able to verify the changes again in our Chrome **Developer tools**:

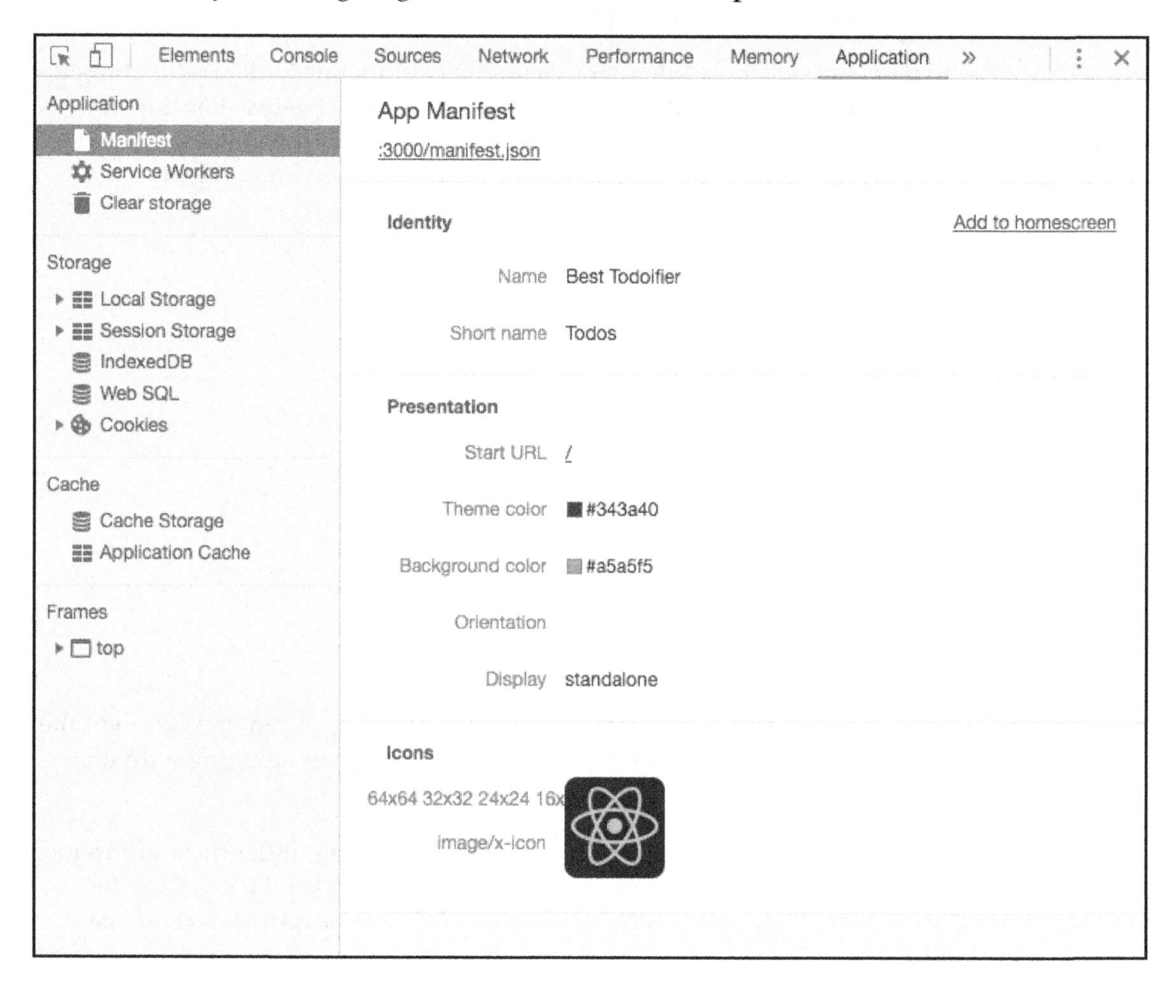

Hooking up Service Workers

The other necessary component to having a working PWA for our application is to build out a Service Worker. Service Workers are another one of those components in PWAs that are not super well-understood, depending on who you ask, and their utility is also not immediately clear. We'll spend a little bit of time exploring and understanding Service Workers, even though the actual amount of work we need to do to implement Service Workers for our PWA is incredibly minimal (maybe even less work than our `manifest` file)!

What is a Service Worker?

Service Workers are defined as a script that your browser runs behind the scenes, separate from the main browser threads. It can intercept network requests, interact with a cache (either storing or retrieving information from a cache), or listen to and deliver push messages. This carries a couple of caveats, too. It is fully asynchronous, so that means anything that requires synchronous operations, such as **XMLHttpRequest** (**XHR**) or operating with **localStorage**, cannot be used inside the Service Worker code. It can also do some other neat tricks, such as receiving push messages even when the app itself is not active, allowing you to display notifications to the user even when the app is not open!

Since it can intercept network requests and store/retrieve information from a server, it can also operate when offline, which allows your application to start up and be used immediately, and progressively fetch updates or update periodically in the background from the server!

The Service Worker life cycle

The life cycle for a Service Worker is pretty simple. There are three main stages:

- Registration
- Installation
- Activation

Each of these stages are pretty self-explanatory.

Registration is the process of letting the browser know where the Service Worker is located and how to install it into the background. The code for registration may look something like this:

```
if ('serviceWorker' in navigator) {
  navigator.serviceWorker.register('/service-worker.js')
  .then(registration => {
    console.log('Service Worker registered!');
   })
  .catch(error => {
    console.log('Error registering service worker! Error is:', error);
   });
}
```

Installation is the process that happens after the Service Worker has been registered, and only happens if the Service Worker either hasn't already been installed, or the Service Worker has changed since the last time.

In a `service-worker.js` file, you'd add something like this to be able to listen to this `event`:

```
self.addEventListener('install', event => {
  // Do something after install
});
```

Finally, **Activation** is the step that happens after all of the other steps have completed. The Service Worker has been registered and then installed, so now it's time for the service worker to start doing its thing:

```
self.addEventListener('activate', event => {
  // Do something upon activation
});
```

How can we use a Service Worker in our app?

So, how do we use a Service Worker in our application? Well, it's simple to do with Create React App, but there is a major caveat: you can't configure the Create React App default generated `service-worker.js` file without ejecting your project, unfortunately! Not all is lost, however; you can still take advantage of some of the highlights of PWAs and service workers by using the default Create React App-generated Service Worker.

To enable this, hop over into `src/index.js`, and, at the final line, change the Service Worker `unregister()` call to `register()` instead:

```
serviceWorker.register();
```

And now we're opting in to our Service Worker! Next, to actually see the results, you'll need to run the following:

```
$ yarn build
```

We'll create a *Production* build (We'll cover this in greater detail in `Chapter 8`, *Getting Your App Ready for Production*). You'll see some output that we'll want to follow as part of this:

```
The build folder is ready to be deployed.
You may serve it with a static server:

  yarn global add serve
  serve -s build
```

As per the instructions, we'll install **serve** globally, and run the command as instructed. When we run this, we should see the following output:

```
$ serve -s build
```

We will get the following output:

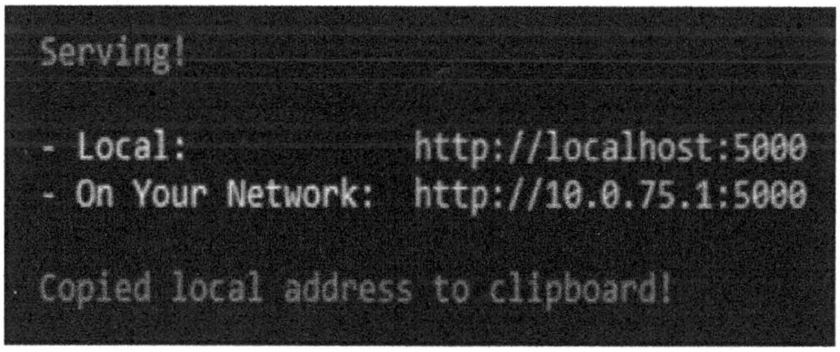

```
Serving!

- Local:            http://localhost:5000
- On Your Network:  http://10.0.75.1:5000

Copied local address to clipboard!
```

Now open up `http://localhost:5000` in your local browser and you'll be able to see, again in the Chrome **Developer tools**, the Service Worker up and running for your application:

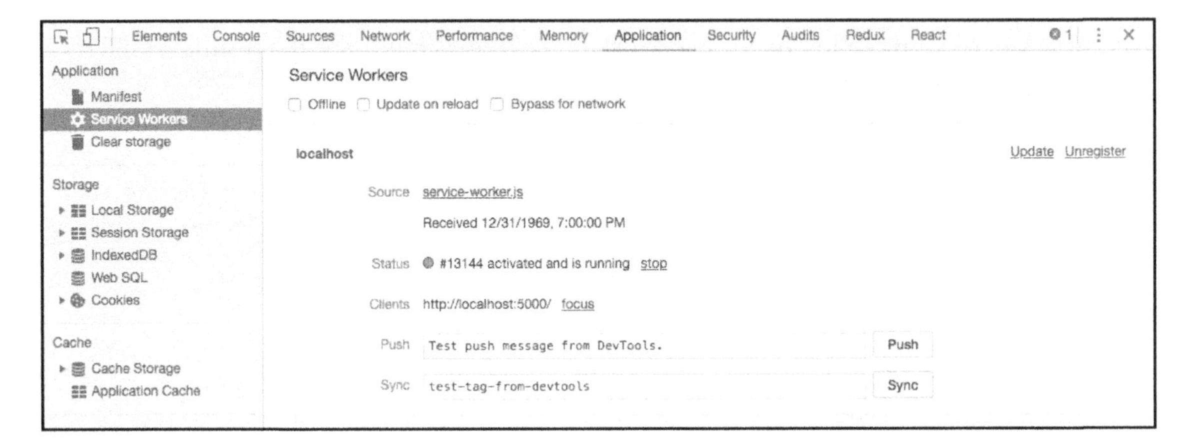

Note that the rule of requiring `HTTPS` for Service Workers and PWAs is not in effect when you're running it on `localhost`!

Summary

Hopefully, we've explored at least enough of Progressive Web Apps that they have at least been partially demystified! A lot of the confusion and trouble with building PWAs tends to stem from the fact that there's not always a good starting point for building one. To get the value out of PWAs, you have to have a PWA, but to build a PWA you typically need to demonstrate the value of them! What a whirlwind!

Create React App limits us a little bit in how we can implement Service Workers, which admittedly limits the functionality and usefulness of our PWA. It doesn't hamstring us, by any means, but doing fun tricks with pre-caching networks and API responses, and loading up our application instantly, even if the browser doing the loading is offline in the first place. That being said, it's like many other things in Create React App: an amazing stepping stone and a great way to get moving with PWAs in the future!

In the next and final chapter, we'll tie up a few loose ends with our project and talk a little bit about production builds and ejecting out of Create React App! We'll look at how to take our code and get it into production. We'll also discuss importing some other major libraries into our Create React App project, such as Redux!

8
Getting Your App Ready for Production

We've put together a pretty nice starter application in Create React App over the span of this book. While it probably won't win any awards, you now have the foundation that you need to be able to build on top of this and turn it into the next world-leading pomodoro tracker, or maybe something like a new task manager application for developers! Throughout all of this, we've covered the build process and the bootstrap process, but have yet to focus on the final portion of building any application: shipping it to production!

We've spent a lot of time talking about the different important features in Create React App, and have built an application on top of it. We've added a lot to our application; we took something from zero to an app that is functional, uses the latest and greatest modern JavaScript programming techniques, and uses the sort of techniques that you'll see when working with Create React App in any sort of professional environment.

We'll need to expand on that and cover the remaining Create React App CLI commands that we can run: `build` and `eject`. We have added a few extra libraries here and there, primarily as utility libraries, but we should also spend a little bit of time working with a few additional libraries, in order to get a feel for how that impacts the workflow. So, we'll discuss a few common libraries, including their usage, impact, and where to go to learn more about them.

By the end of this chapter, you will have learned about the following topics:

- Adding other libraries to our application
- Using Create React App `eject`, and its impact on your application
- Using Create React App `build` to create a production build

Adding other libraries

As we mentioned previously, we'll be adding a few more libraries. If you're not interested in swapping either of these libraries, you can safely skip this section, but there are a few items to cover that may be representative of scenarios that you'll run into while working on JavaScript in a team environment. For example, Redux was, at one point, considered important (if not essential) for building a React project of any significant complexity. Recently, that mentality has ebbed a bit, and generally speaking, people will only opt for using libraries like Redux when it is more necessary and state management is a harder part of their applications. Regardless, we should have experience in adding it to our applications, so that we will be ready to contribute, should we ever be working on a project that is using it as well. There are a lot of other common libraries that people use in conjunction with React, and we'll cover them very quickly here, before moving on to a quick example of using Redux in a Create React App project!

Other popular React libraries

There are other libraries that come up frequently when working with React. These may be libraries that help you to use your browser's address bar to figure out what component to render as its main application, or they may be libraries that give any form elements that you use in React a little more native functionality and remove more boilerplate code.

React Router

React Router is a library aimed at helping you route requests to particular components. The idea is that when someone visits your project, they may want to interact with a specific component. This helps you to manage those requests and figure out the right way to get the user directly to that component. The good news is that installing React Router and using it inside of a Create React App project is actually pretty simple! To install it, all you need to run is the following command:

```
$ yarn add react-router-dom
```

Then, you can modify your `src/App/App.js` file to start adding new routes to components! React Router is similar to Redux, in that it is an incredibly complex project by itself; so, if you want to learn more, you can visit `https://reacttraining.com/react-router/`.

React Final Form

Odds are, if you're working with any form of interactive web application, you'll need to be able to handle web forms in a consistent and performant way. The great news is that, because this is such a common problem, there are a number of popular libraries out there to handle dealing with forms in React efficiently. The most popular of these is React Final Form, which you can add to your project by running the following command:

```
$ yarn add react-final-form final-form
```

From there, you can use any of React Final Form's functionality to replace the forms in your application! For more information on how to properly take advantage of this library, you can visit `https://github.com/final-form/react-final-form`.

Adding Redux for state management

Redux is a common library for managing the state of your application, especially when it is a little more complicated, and you want to control the flow of events in your frontend project! Redux provides a way for you to tightly control how the entire state of your application is affected by different types of events, such as button clicks or form changes. If your application gets incredibly large and complex, and managing too many different streams of events affecting your application becomes too hard, it is a great time to introduce something like Redux to your project!

The good news is that, similar to the previous libraries, you can also add Redux to your Create React App project without a lot of extra fuss! You'll want both `redux` and `react-redux`, to make sure that you have all of the bindings that you'd normally need to connect everything together:

```
$ yarn add redux react-redux
```

This should install everything that you need to get started with Redux. Similar to the other libraries that we've mentioned, Redux is an incredibly complex topic that could easily fill up an entire book by itself. If you'd like to learn more about Redux, visit `https://redux.js.org/`.

Creating a production build

Finally, we're ready to get this all bundled up and ready for a production deployment! Our code is done, our code works, and everything is great; so, what do we do now?

It's simple; we just run `yarn build` and call it a day! Well, that's most of the process. You see, when you run `yarn build`, Create React App tries to figure out the best, most efficient way to bundle up everything that you've been working on in your Create React App project and minify/productionize everything that you've written—every image and asset that you've added, every library that needs to be included—everything.

How to create a production build

To create a production build, we just need to run `yarn build`. It's that simple! See the following:

```
$ yarn build
yarn run v1.12.3
$ react-scripts build
Creating an optimized production build...
Compiled successfully.

File sizes after gzip:

69.67 KB (+4.53 KB) build/static/js/1.877dc59d.chunk.js
21.85 KB build/static/css/1.4cb1c3c1.chunk.css
2.32 KB (+46 B) build/static/js/main.1f5d1459.chunk.js
763 B build/static/js/runtime~main.229c360f.js
507 B build/static/css/main.af121e46.chunk.css

The project was built assuming it is hosted at the server root.
You can control this with the homepage field in your package.json.
For example, add this to build it for GitHub Pages:

"homepage" : "http://myname.github.io/myapp",

The build folder is ready to be deployed.
You may serve it with a static server:

yarn global add serve
serve -s build

Find out more about deployment here:

http://bit.ly/CRA-deploy

Done in 26.70s.
```

You should now have a production-ready build of files in the `build/` directory of your application! This is a heavily-optimized build, ready to be copied and deployed, wherever you can deploy your application!

What's important to note is that the output of this process are static files (fully compiled HTML/JS/CSS) that can be deployed and run from any place that can serve static files back to a user—so, essentially, any kind of **content delivery network** (**CDN**) or web server that you may already have.

This process relies heavily on Webpack's build process and multiple different build and optimization plugins that optimize nearly every part of the build process. Files are minified, chunked by their usage and scope (to reduce importing files that we don't need), and set up in a way that allows for browser caching, to reduce as much effort as possible each time a person revisits your site!

Minified means that the files are reduced down in file size as much as possible, by renaming code, minimizing whitespace, or otherwise cutting down on extraneous code, so that the amount of JavaScript that needs to be deployed is as small as possible.

Thoughts on the deployment process

The actual deployment process is a little bit more tricky. There are a million and one ways to deploy this, but as we have built our application off of a proxy backend server, one of the methods is for us to integrate our project into an existing backend server with something to serve our frontend code from, such as a Rails/node/Phoenix server. This allows us to run this code as our frontend and have a backend server behind the scenes, powering this application. Without that, our app won't work; as you may recall, this is an application powered by a `Todo` backend.

Ejecting our project

One of the other options available to us is the ability to `eject` our project in Create React App. **Ejecting** an app means that it removes all of the scaffolds and confines of the Create React App CLI, with all of the bonuses and caveats that you might expect from such an operation. For one, we gain greater ability and control over our project, and can tweak things as we see fit, which is great; but it also puts you into a world where you need to understand your Babel configs, your Webpack configs, and every other behind the scenes configuration option that you were previously able to ignore.

Eject is very much a double-edged sword; it's a powerful tool, and it allows you to move beyond the rules that Create React App introduces into your world. However, you'll now be responsible for any headaches that come as a result of configuration modifications in the future.

That being said, `eject` is also an important command in the Create React App world. I've seen many projects that started off with a Create React App built project, but changed when the app became sufficiently complex. At that point, ejecting is a good idea, in order to be able to appropriately tweak things as you need to. Again, a big focus of this book is to understand how to become an expert on Create React App and its latest version; so, understanding and using all of the commands is a major part of that.

How to eject

Let's start by talking about how to perform an `eject` with Create React App. The process itself is actually simple enough: you just run `npm run eject` or `yarn eject`, and the process begins. This is also not quite enough information to be able to make an informed decision about when and where to `eject` with Create React App, so we'll actually explore the results of running the command. We'll start off by moving this into a new branch in our source control of choice (or, if you're not using one, copy the directory somewhere, so that you can play with this without fear of losing your project).

This is a permanent operation. If you don't want to be stuck with these changes, ensure that you have copied your folder, or branched it in such a way that you don't get locked into an `eject` during this section!

We get the following output:

```
$ yarn eject

yarn run v1.12.3
$ react-scripts eject
? Are you sure you want to eject? This action is permanent. (y/N)
If you answer yes, you'll see a ton of output:

Ejecting...

Copying files into /Users/brandon/Documents/dev/create-react-app-
book/code/todoifier
Adding /config/env.js to the project
Adding /config/paths.js to the project
Adding /config/webpack.config.dev.js to the project
```

```
Adding /config/webpack.config.prod.js to the project
Adding /config/webpackDevServer.config.js to the project
Adding /config/jest/cssTransform.js to the project
Adding /config/jest/fileTransform.js to the project
Adding /scripts/build.js to the project
Adding /scripts/start.js to the project
Adding /scripts/test.js to the project

Updating the dependencies
Removing react-scripts from dependencies
Adding ...lots of packages... to dependencies

Updating the scripts
Replacing "react-scripts start" with "node scripts/start.js"
Replacing "react-scripts build" with "node scripts/build.js"
Replacing "react-scripts test" with "node scripts/test.js"

Configuring package.json
Adding Jest configuration
Adding Babel preset
Adding ESLint configuration

Running yarn...
[1/4] Resolving packages...
[2/4] Fetching packages...
[3/4] Linking dependencies...
[4/4] Building fresh packages...

success Saved lockfile.
Ejected successfully!

Please consider sharing why you ejected in this survey:
http://goo.gl/forms/Bi6CZjk1EqsdelXk1

Done in 14.39s.
```

Wow! A lot happens when you `eject`! It creates roughly 13 new scripts, most of which are either helper/utility JavaScript files or configuration files for things like Webpack, Babel, or Jest. A lot of this is the process of allowing you to continue to use your project as if it were already a major Create React App project, despite the fact that you just ejected. For example, most of our commands should work identically. If I run `yarn test`, for example, I should still get a full `Test Suite` running and passing:

```
$ yarn test
yarn run v1.12.3
node scripts/test.js
```

```
PASS src/NewTodo/NewTodo.test.js
PASS src/TodoList/TodoList.test.js
PASS src/Todo/Todo.test.js
PASS src/App/App.test.js

Test Suites: 4 passed, 4 total
Tests: 21 passed, 21 total
Snapshots: 3 passed, 3 total
Time: 5.939s
Ran all test suites.

Watch Usage: Press w to show more.
```

Similarly, if I run `yarn start`, I should be able to expect to use my React project in the same way that I always have:

```
$ yarn run v1.12.3
node scripts/start.js
```

Our browser should still spin up and open itself to `http://localhost:3000/`. We can also continue to run our own backend simulation server, with requests getting proxied appropriately! As you can see, the Create React App team did everything they could to make `eject` as painless and seamless a process as it possibly could be. We can even still build for production with `yarn build`.

We can also see the configuration files that are created for us, based on how Create React App structures its projects. We can see the Webpack configs, for example, in these files:

```
Adding /config/webpack.config.dev.js to the project
Adding /config/webpack.config.prod.js to the project
```

If you wanted to tweak your `config` in some custom way, this is where you'd do it, and you can base your configs off of the incredibly elaborate files that they've populated here.

You can also see how they've set up Jest to work so seamlessly, by looking at the scripts folder for `scripts/test.js`, as well as the Jest-specific configuration files located in `config/`.

Drawbacks of using eject

Remember that this does not all come for free, and there's no reason not to just immediately `eject` a project. First off, you will not get any potential time-saving changes or productivity enhancers when the Create React App team updates the scripts for Create React App. You'll be in your own world if something breaks, if something doesn't work right, or otherwise, and you won't really have anywhere to reach out to for support.

The `eject` command is like buying something as-is. It might not have any strings attached to it anymore, but it also doesn't have any support, either. Buyer beware!

Summary

That's it! At this point, you should have a solid grasp of Create React App 2's changes and benefits. We've explored functionality, both old and new, to make sure that we're building the most up-to-date, modern JavaScript implementations that we possibly can! We're using libraries and techniques that we would already be using in most frontend projects that we might build.

We've also taken a deep dive into how to set up a healthy software development life cycle using Create React App, getting us to a point where our application runs smoothly and is resilient when changes do occur. Our application is well and thoroughly tested, and is not prone to random breaking. This is all something that we've done with absolutely zero configuration; in my mind, this is one of the biggest strengths of working with a frontend development project in Create React App!

We've also integrated a number of other non-specific Create React App solutions into our code, whether it is better CSS support through CSS modules or SASS, or additional libraries and clever abstractions via service libraries. We've striven to code our projects in a smart way that allows for easy reuse and expandability, without making our projects obtuse or difficult for other developers to contribute to. We've also proxied a backend API, so that we can work with backend developers and show them the interface and data language that the frontend uses, reducing the friction and back-and-forth between multiple development teams and ideologies!

Finally, you've seen what our options become when we outgrow the safe confines of Create React App and eject our application into a standard Webpack configuration! Our application lives on, and we can configure new and exciting additions to our project without hobbling ourselves or our development team!

I hope you've learned a lot about how to really get started with Create React App (and, by proxy, React itself). Thank you so much for coming with me on this journey, and I can't wait to see what you build out there!

Other Books You May Enjoy

If you enjoyed this book, you may be interested in these other books by Packt:

React and React Native
Adam Boduch

ISBN: 9781786465658

- Craft reusable React components
- Control navigation using the React Router to help keep your UI in sync with URLs
- Build isomorphic web applications using Node.js
- Use the Flexbox layout model to create responsive mobile designs
- Leverage the native APIs of Android and iOS to build engaging applications with React Native
- Respond to gestures in a way that's intuitive for the user
- Use Relay to build a unified data architecture for your React UIs

Full-Stack React Projects
Shama Hoque

ISBN: 9781788835534

- Set up your development environment and develop a MERN application
- Implement user authentication and authorization using JSON Web Tokens
- Build a social media application by extending the basic MERN application
- Create an online marketplace application with shopping cart and Stripe payments
- Develop a media streaming application using MongoDB GridFS
- Implement server-side rendering with data to improve SEO
- Set up and use React 360 to develop user interfaces with VR capabilities
- Learn industry best practices to make MERN stack applications reliable and scalable

Leave a review - let other readers know what you think

Please share your thoughts on this book with others by leaving a review on the site that you bought it from. If you purchased the book from Amazon, please leave us an honest review on this book's Amazon page. This is vital so that other potential readers can see and use your unbiased opinion to make purchasing decisions, we can understand what our customers think about our products, and our authors can see your feedback on the title that they have worked with Packt to create. It will only take a few minutes of your time, but is valuable to other potential customers, our authors, and Packt. Thank you!

Index

R

S

T

X

Made in the USA
Coppell, TX
26 October 2021

64705283R00105